Are Schools Really Like This?

Factors Affecting Teacher Attitude
toward School Improvement

INNOVATIONS IN SCIENCE EDUCATION AND TECHNOLOGY

Series Editor:

Karen C. Cohen, Harvard University, Cambridge, Massachusetts

A Continuation Order Plan is available for this series. A continuation order will bring delivery of each new volume immediately upon publication. Volumes are billed only upon actual shipment. For further information please contact the publisher.

Are Schools Really Like This?

Factors Affecting Teacher Attitude toward School Improvement

J. Gary Lilyquist

Independent Quality Consultant in Education
Milltown, Wisconsin

PLENUM PRESS • NEW YORK AND LONDON

Library of Congress Cataloging-in-Publication Data

Lilyquist, J. Gary
    Are schools really like this? : factors affecting teacher attitude toward school
improvement / J. Gary Lilyquist.
        p.   cm. — (Innovations in science education and technology)
    Includes bibliographical references and index.
    ISBN 0-306-45735-0
    1. School improvement programs—United States—Case studies. 2. Teachers—United
States—Attitudes—Case studies. 3. School environment—United States—Case studies.
4. Teacher participation in administration—United States—Case studies. I. Title.
II. Series
LB2822.82.L55 1998   97-40389
371.1'06—dc21   CIP

ISBN 0-306-45735-0

© 1998 Plenum Press, New York
A Division of Plenum Publishing Corporation
233 Spring Street, New York, N.Y. 10013

http://www.plenum.com

10 9 8 7 6 5 4 3 2 1

Printed in the United States of America

This book is dedicated to the improvement of
learning opportunities for all children

Foreword

This is a hopeful book with a message that should cheer those who have devoted their lives to public schools. It emphatically states that the system should be saved, although it affirms that change is needed. It is about how to reconcile differing visions of school through an understanding of what is involved in the working of schools and of the nature of change.

The book's several strengths make it useful both to readers who are school people as well as to those who are not. It really does describe what schools are like through a deep and detailed discussion of three case studies. It actually brings systems thinking and a review of the research into school work in an attempt to analyze how to make needed and lasting changes.

Its personal, interactive style engages the reader in a conversation about how to change schools to improve student learning. It ventures into the realm of teacher status while clearly warning us not to blame the people. It stresses the complexity of the institution and its interdependence with its client groups.

It is clearly a book by someone who respects and enjoys working with schools and the people who are connected with them.

Isa Kaftal Zimmerman, Superintendent
Acton Public Schools
Acton-Boxborough Regional School District
Acton, Massachusetts

Preface

Systems thinking, already an established movement in many businesses and industries, has only recently been introduced into the educational system. This book is intended to provide a framework for educators, teachers-in-training, educational administrators, parents, community members, government leadership, and policy makers. To successfully carry out school improvements, the framework combines the concepts of systems thinking, mental models, effective school research, and Quality Management Theory. Using analysis of six organizational dimensions (internal and external cultures, leadership, strategy, structure, and results), three case studies show the attempts of school systems to balance the culture's visions of a good school. The book also comments on how these individuals and groups could apply more systems thinking.

The examples of three school cultures that are likely to be familiar to the reader offer a different way to approach school improvement. First, the book offers in a systemic format a rationale as to why people react (positively and negatively) to school improvement. Second, it compares three case studies that support suggestions of why schools are not improving. Third, it suggests a new approach, a Balance Alignment Model, for systemic school improvement. The concluding chapters discuss three key boundaries that cannot be ignored if we want to carry out successful projects to increase student learning. Otherwise these boundaries may contradict popular ideas about how to improve our schools.

Acknowledgments

Three people have had great influence on me, shaping my thinking on management theory and leading to completion of this book. First, Professor Jacob O. Stampen, Department of Educational Administration, University of Wisconsin-Madison, offered continued guidance and a nonjudgmental style of teaching, creating a learning condition in which I was free to explore and challenge my mental model on management theory. Second, Professor B. Dean Bowles challenged my understanding of Quality Management Theory and its compatibility with education's political system. Third, Professor Mark P. Finster, Grainger School of Business, in the Center for Quality and Productivity Improvement, introduced me to the Masters of Quality Improvement Theory.

I value the opportunity to have worked with Dr. Betty B. Hoskins, the Developmental Editor. She was very helpful and supportive of changes in the text.

Without the support of JoAnne, I would not have had the opportunity to write this book.

Contents

Introduction

In 1992 I thought, "there must be a better way to manage schools." Four years earlier, I had been appointed chief executive officer of a preschool through 12th grade school district, in a rural community in the upper midwest. The district's financial condition was poor, buildings were in need of repair, test scores were below the state average, and plans to meet state-mandated requirements were behind by 3 years. My charge was to bring the school finances under control, upgrade the buildings, raise test scores, and improve the school climate. I knew that this would be a long and difficult process, and would require the involvement of many people—teachers, support staff, parents, and community members—in making important decisions. Over the course of 4 years, I used information from school research that suggested intense involvement of people in the decision-making process. By 1992, the district seemed a different place. The buildings were clean and well-maintained, teachers had more instructional supplies, test scores had risen each year, and the cost per student had increased by less than half the state's average.

A core curriculum committee, comprised of teachers and community members, had full control of curriculum development. Each year, three or four curriculum areas were reviewed and updated by a team of kindergarten through 12th grade teachers, parents, and community members. Each team met on a regular schedule during the school day to write curriculum. Planning and curriculum review meeting times were set to accommodate the members' schedules. Teachers and support staff selected and attended district-wide in-service programs, which enabled them to upgrade skills, earn college credit, and advance on the salary schedule. The school board became more efficient, holding shorter meetings and settling contracts for teachers and support staff in one or two sessions rather than 2 or 3 years.

In only four years, I believed I had accomplished my goals by involving people in decision-making. If this sounds too good to be true, it was!

Three years after I had begun to implement changes in the district, teachers rebelled. They were angry that they were taken out of their classrooms so often for in-service training, and that they had to use new methods of instruction (even though the methods had been recommended by the teachers themselves). A specialty teacher began to hold secret meetings with parents to pressure the school board to return to textbook instruction. A group of community members began to criticize both me and the seven-member board, claiming that the board was not providing adequate leadership during its short meetings. Two members left the board voluntarily; two of the five remaining members were voted out of office.

I was in shock. The literature said, involve people, use participatory management with strategic planning, do your best to supply teachers with what they need, empower teachers, provide opportunities for rewards, work with the union to solve labor problems, try to align district goals with individual goals, and express good news. I had done all of these things, but no one—including me—was happy.

The changes I implemented did improve student learning, but at a high cost. Many people were dissatisfied with the changes. Why? I didn't know. Thus began my journey to discover what had gone wrong. I wanted to find a way to improve student learning outcomes while maintaining support of the teachers and the community. I undertook doctoral studies, during which I studied three school systems. I gave fictional names to the three communities I studied in order to track their unique characteristics. This book explains why my attempt to "follow the rules" of the school improvement literature floundered. I discovered that I was not alone in my dilemma. Our society has built an educational structure that actually *prevents* school improvement by pointing the finger of blame rather than finding the root causes of problems. The finger-pointing drives fear into people and causes them to retreat to a defensive, isolated "survival mode" that rejects risk. But improvement requires risk-taking. In effect, the current educational structure forces teachers to resist change and to protect their vision of a good classroom. Improving our schools requires us to know more about the frontiers of systems thinking pioneered by W. Edwards Deming, Joseph M. Juran, and others, and to apply this knowledge to the total educational system. In this book, I offer a new way to think about school improvement, in the hope that others will be able to avoid my mistakes, and will be able to improve our schools without generating so much resistance from teachers, support staff, parents, and community members.

This book describes the activities and processes that contribute to "survival mentality" and that can build more positive individual and community visions of schools. Chapter 2 introduces systems thinking, which suggests that both forces internal to the school, and actions and processes outside the school's control, create patterns of interrelationships. Each individual action or process affects the whole system. This concept is supported by Senge (1994, 1990), Barker (1992), Juran (1992), Glasser (1990a,b, 1984), and Deming (1986) who are theorists on systems thinking. Chapters 3 and 4 provide a systems model of naturally occurring events. The model describes several organizational dimensions—leadership, strategy, structure, and results—that react to innovation in an attempt to balance the internal and external visions of a school. Chapters 5 through 12 explain what can occur in each dimension to place a "stranglehold" on improvements. Chapter 13 suggests how the knowledge of systems thinking can be applied to school improvement.

RESEARCH METHOD

The method for research was guided by the Ground Theory approach of Glaser and Strauss (1967). Factors that explain teacher attitude toward school improvement were explored across six institutional dimensions: external environment culture, internal environment culture, leadership, strategy, structure, and results. Taken together, these dimensions constitute a "universe" of possible influences.

For political sociogram development Glaser and Strauss's approach was combined with Bowles's (1993a,b) method. Bowles uses data to identify factors in individual, group, or institutional behaviors. Data collected in this study were compared: to establish customary interaction, activities, values and/or sentiments; to compare who interacted with whom; to establish patterns of influence; to translate patterns of influence into a sociogram. After additional observations, the sociograms were modified. Modification continued until the data verified the lines of influence between individuals, groups, and the institution. The result produced a final sociogram, which identified key individuals and groups influencing school activities.

USING THIS BOOK

Our plans to improve our schools are limited by boundaries, whether we recognize them or not. This book outlines three key boundaries that we cannot ignore if we want to carry out successful projects to increase student learning. These boundaries result from key factors (or patterns) that affect teachers' attitudes toward school improvement. The factors are educational innovations or changes in organizational structure that: (1) modify a teacher's rank in the social structure, (2) block teachers from gaining status or place them at risk of losing status, and (3) run contrary to what the teacher perceives as his or her vision.

These factors create boundaries, which may contradict popular ideas about how to improve student learning. You will be introduced to the successes and failures of Dryden School's restructuring plan, which disrupted the school's culture. You will meet the Elkin principal who said that he could not change his school's culture because he could not bring in teachers with new ideas or perspective on education. The principal and teachers worked two or more hours beyond the regular school day, scarcely a "selling point" for more innovation. This principal's problem was representative of the administrative perspective on hiring. All administrators face boundaries that restrict their actions, whether they like them or not. The three key factors seem rigid and unworkable, but it is possible to make changes without crossing the boundaries they represent.

The Balance Alignment Model can be used to guide the development of strategies to improve student learning. The balance portion of the model suggests that if a new strategy throws the system too far out of balance, it generates actions that block implementation of the innovation. Would-be innovators must study the cultures of both the external and internal environments, and determine the boundaries of the improvement project, the points at which the project threatens existing visions of a good school or classroom. You will be introduced to Skyland's attempt to improve its schools. One part of the community embraced the structural changes; another part actively attempted to block them. Neither group had baseline data that supported its position. In addition, the planning group neglected to use data related to student learning, and did not know what kind of data would convince community groups that the changes had improved the schools. Ultimately, any results could be used to "prove" anyone's "gut feelings," which may or may not be related to increases in student learning. The tampering process produced a divided community with no certainty about the impact of structural changes on student learning.

The three case studies provide a framework that individuals or groups in the external and internal environments can use to find key patterns of agreement and disagreement about their visions of a good school. In both cultures, the formal and informal leadership hold the responsibility for blocking or carrying out innovations. At least one of these leadership groups must initiate changes in the ineffective tampering process. Whichever leadership group takes this "heroic step," it must anticipate attempts by other leadership groups to block its actions. Its strategies must include plans to build the support of threatened groups. This takes time, because the threatened groups must be allowed to hold their own ideas about how schools can be improved. Mental models regarding school improvement can and do change over time, but there are fragile boundaries that control how fast the planning group can advance before its efforts are blocked.

Although this book offers many examples of how efforts at improving schools are blocked, each community and school organization has its unique stories. You must apply the ideas in this book to your knowledge of human behaviors and the use of power, and combine the results with continuous improvement practices and effective schools research, to find the key patterns in your own community that will block or enhance school improvement.

Remember that the longest journey begins with a single step. This is true, also, of meaningful school improvement. A single person—you—can begin to use systems thinking to improve learning for all children. Using systems think-ing, you can encourage others to work within boundaries and discover the key patterns that control your school system. Then you will be able to release the stranglehold one step at a time.

While struggling to write this book, my son wrote a note of encouragement to me. Jeremy wrote, "Once past the fear of failure there is nothing else to do, but to succeed."

Good luck in applying systems thinking!

CHAPTER 1

Vision of a Good School

"Are schools really like this?" That was the first comment I received about the first draft of this book. I knew that the answer, for the schools I had studied, was *"Yes."* But a second comment, by a Chapter One teacher who works with students who score low in reading and/or math, was even more meaningful. *"You studied our school!"* she insisted. *"How did you find out these things?"*

My response was that schools are more similar than we may recognize. I have never been in the Chapter One teacher's school, but she thought I had revealed its secrets. And the secrets—as I had learned from the first and second reactions—contradicted common public beliefs about our schools. I urge the readers, compare the information offered in this book with their own visions of a school.

You, the readers, are among the many people who want schools to improve and are willing to help improve them. For you, my main goal is to change your approach to school improvement, and thus to help you match your school with your vision of a school.

New evidence suggests that many of the actions taken to improve schools are slowly strangling them (Lilyquist, 1995). Current critics ask, "Who is strangling our schools? Who is to blame?" But the rational approach, the question based on fact would ask, "What factors are causing the stranglehold on schools?" This is a question that rational people can study and attempt to answer.

The evidence presented in this book suggests that *the way schools conduct their business* creates barriers to school improvement. This book calls that way of conducting business "the system."

So, we must understand the system. Not just one part of the system, such as "the teachers" or "the administrators" or "the school board," but rather the *whole* system. The entire system is affected by the actions of each part. Thus, a key to understanding the stranglehold is understanding why people act as they do in relationship to the way schools as *systems* carry out the business of educating students.

Individuals' actions and reactions to changes in schools and to the results schools produce are based on their vision of a good school. Each of us has a

7

vision of a good school, which may or may not be the same vision held by our next-door neighbor, or teachers, or the school board, or residents of another community. These variations in vision are not "bad"; they are simply examples of the differences that define us as individuals, as members of a group, or as a community. If you want to check this out, ask yourself, "What is my vision of a good school?" Write down your answer. Now ask one or more individuals from a different culture or different part of your community to tell you their visions of a good school. You may be surprised at the differences and similarities.

How does a personal vision affect schools? As individuals, members of groups, and community residents, we use our vision of a good school to judge the results our schools produce. Depending on whether the results support or threaten our particular vision of the school, we decide whether or not to take supporting or opposing action.

THE TEACHERS' PARADOX

As I interviewed teachers and then observed their actions. I realized that people react in accordance with their vision. When I asked teachers if they wanted to work in schools that focused on improving student learning, they all responded that they did. (Of course, this is the answer we hope for!) I then asked the teachers, "How does your school operate compared to attributes that describe a school focused on improving student learning?" Teachers reported a significant gap between what they would like to see and how their schools operated. In general, they wanted to work in schools that improved student learning, and they thought their own schools could do a better job of this important task.

But when I asked the same teachers to describe how they used their time, they reported spending a significant portion of it to maintain their own power, to build their own status by reaping rewards, and to protect their own well-being. (Do not prejudge the teachers' response, or let it make you angry. As you'll discover, these are perfectly rational uses of time in the current political structure under which our educational system functions.) Teachers said they wanted to work in schools that focused on improving student learning; they reported using their time on self-preservation issues: power, status, rewards, and well-being. This is a paradox.

This paradox raises a new question. Why would teachers focus on self-preservation more than on improving student learning? The short answer is that schools are too politically driven and unstructured to offer teachers much real choice in their behavior. Remember the teachers' vision of a good school: one that focuses on improving student learning. Teachers act through the political structure of the school to protect themselves *because only by protecting themselves can they protect their vision of a good classroom.* As you will find, the system has taught teachers this is the only safe way to act.

All but a few teachers see this paradox themselves. Evidence (Lilyquist, 1995; Conzemius, 1993) suggests that it exists for all teachers, whether or not they realize it. All teachers need to maintain power, status, rewards, and a level of well-being, in order to control their own classrooms. The few teachers who claim not to be concerned about self-preservation issues, and who maintain that the paradox simply does not exist, already have sufficient power to control and protect their vision. My observations suggest that these teachers do indeed use their time to maintain their power, gaining status through rewards; this protects both their sense of well-being and their vision of a good classroom.

Why is it necessary to understand this paradox in order to implement school improvements and ultimately to improve student learning? Many people expect teachers to place students' interests ahead of their own. Parents, public officials, and school administrators assume that teachers will not hesitate to carry out innovations that promise to improve student learning. Paradoxically, however, teachers will resist innovations—however important to student learning—that appear to threaten their own interests. Any effort to improve schools may thus be undermined if administrators and community members do not understand this paradox.

The implication that teachers might inadvertently undermine any program that promises to improve student learning is particularly disturbing. The question this book attempts to answer is: Do teachers assign a higher priority to their individual visions of how students should be educated than to a more collective vision that emerges from external mandates and administrative initiatives?

I do not assign blame to teachers who act to protect their own self-interests. My research indicates that virtually every teacher works hard, wants to teach, and wants children to learn and to improve, according to his or her own vision of a good classroom. Teachers try their best to protect their individual vision against real and perceived threats, and this constitutes the paradox.

THE PARADOX AND THE COMMUNITY

Before we can fully understand and change the paradoxical behavior of teachers, we need to understand the actions of parents and others in the community with regard to their schools. Parents, other individuals in the local community, community groups, and representatives at all levels of government react to the results school produce. Each of these actors is compelled to respond to gaps between perceived results and his or her personal or collective visions of a good school.

Many of the results salient to parents, community members, community groups, and government representatives have nothing directly to do with improving student learning. For example, decisions to build new schools, or to remodel or sell old school buildings, may cause the community to react either positively or negatively toward school authorities. Similarly, community members may react negatively or positively to a decision that restructures the school district and changes the use of a particular school buildings; for example, making a former K-through-sixth-grade elementary school into a K-through-third-grade school will be a subject of community discussion. Decisions related to finances, labor contracts, and school employees' behavior can all excite an active response by parents, other community members, community organizations, or government representatives.

Of course, results that seem to measure student achievement directly, such as dropout rates, state and national test scores, and parents' or communities' perceptions of an individual child's performance, also affect community response. Often, these results are based on very little data, or data that are misinterpreted. In many cases, it does not matter whether results truly reflect changes in student learning. Parents, community members, community groups, and all individuals at levels of government will attempt to *control* the local school in order to protect their own (possibly conflicting) visions of a good school.

VISIONS AND MISSIONS

When we combine our knowledge of what teachers protect (their visions of a good classroom) and what members of the public protect (their visions of a good school), it is easy to understand why schools do not have a common mission. Of course, most schools do have written mission statements. However, when teachers, administrators, parents, community members, and governing officials in the same community are asked, "What is your school's mission?" they come to no common consensus.

In the past, local schools did have a common, and commonly understood, mission. Until the 1950s, most local communities held common values, beliefs, norms, and mores. These defined the local schools' mission. Schools and school teachers knew what the community expected them to teach, and they willingly accepted the community's mandates when their social beliefs were aligned with the community. Over the past three to seven decades, several forces have combined to change this situation. Influences outside local community control (the global economy, state and federal mandates, and so forth) define the schools' mission. A highly mobile society has radically increased diversity within communities, causing a clash of cultural values, beliefs, norms, and mores. As a result, local communities often cannot agree on what schools should or should not do. When local community members and school personnel disagree about the schools' mission, individuals and small groups within the community work even harder to protect and implement their own visions of a good school. The fragmented, disconnected visions held by individuals and groups in the community move them to actions that create and perpetuate the stranglehold on schools.

This concept of individual reactions based on individual visions for schools is not new. Peter Senge (1994, 1990), Joel Barker (1992), and William Glasser (1990a,b, 1984), three contemporary writers on schools and organizational improvement, use similar images to describe how and why people react to changes in schools and other organizations. Glasser's Control Theory suggests that people have a "picture album" in their mind based on past experiences. Individuals use their albums to explain what is around them and to adjust their behavior accordingly. Glasser claims that people cannot be forced, mandated, or coerced into behaviors that do not match pictures in their album. He argues that if people are to react differently, they must first allow their pictures to change. In short, people will resist what they do not understand, what is contrary to the pictures in their album.

Peter Senge describes individual vision as "mental models." He writes that "mental models are deeply ingrained assumptions, generalizations, or even pictures or images that influence how we understand the world and how we take action" (p. 8). He believes that in order to change how we act, we have to turn inward. We have to learn to unearth our internal pictures of the world. By bringing our mental models to the surface, we expose what we have been taught; this opens us to the influence of others. (This book will use Senge's terminology.)

Joel Barker would call these concepts "paradigms." He argues that individuals or organizations must change their paradigms in order to explore new possibilities and contribute to growth, at both the individual and organizational levels.

Resistance to change appears to be based on deep-seated visions of the world. Glasser, Senge, and Barker agree that we are controlled by our own "picture albums," our "mental models," our "paradigms" of the world. If people are to change their visions, they must change their mental pictures, or exchange old pictures for new ones.

But how are mental models created? We build them gradually, incrementally, from what we see and feel every day. As our mental models are reinforced by daily events, they become stronger and harder to change.

Let's return to the question, "What creates the stranglehold on schools?" All of the events related to schools, to which individuals in a community have been exposed, are a system of interrelated events. These have caused individuals to build their own mental images, which create their visions of a school. These, in turn, control the ways individuals act and react toward school improvement. The total system thus contributes to building diverse and possibly conflicting visions of a good school. The stranglehold is in the incongruities of these inner images or visions.

Return, for a moment, to the teachers' paradox. The teachers want to improve student learning, but the system has taught individual teachers that the only way to protect this vision is to control their own classrooms. Thus, a physical education teacher, a special education teacher, a guidance counselor, and a regular classroom teacher all describe their behaviors as the result of "survival mentality." What is it about the system that causes these educators to focus on survival?

Three key factors affect teachers' attitudes toward any educational innovations or organizational changes: (1) modifications to a teacher's rank in the social structure, (2) restrictions that block teachers from gaining status or place them at risk of losing status, and (3) concepts that contradict the teacher's vision of a good classroom. Affecting these will be considered in later chapters.

CHAPTER 2

Systems Thinking

Systems thinking goes beyond standard organizational charts that establish a hierarchical structure defining who is on top and on bottom to define the schools' work flow, patterns of interrelationship, and processes. Organizational charts can explain the chain of command or lay out prescribed steps in a set of connected events, but anyone who works in a school knows that both the chain of command and prescribed procedures are sometimes ignored. Why? Because there are other forces at work that change people's behavior. These may include mental picture albums, mental models, paradigms, and visions and influences beyond the control of individuals or organizations (Senge, 1994; Barker, 1992; Glasser, 1990a,b, 1984).

These forces make up the "systemic structure," an all-inclusive structure for understanding the operations of a complex system such as a school or a school district. Although systemic structures operate in every complex system, they are often invisible until someone notices and explains them. This is where systems thinking comes in: the consideration of interrelationships among what is known, known incorrectly, unknown and unknowable, visible and invisible, already explored and yet to be discovered. Systems thinking allows you to understand causes and effects that are beyond your direct control, and ultimately to enhance the forces that support school improvement and attempt to mitigate the forces that create barriers. As Edwards Deming (1993, 1986) has said, "We must manage the unknown and unknowable."

Using systems thinking, you can discover key patterns of interrelationships so that you can focus your attention on them. No one individual has the time—or the ability—to manage all of the parts of a complex system. You can optimize your use of time by managing only key patterns that have extensive effects on the system. Systems thinking makes it more obvious how one person's actions affect others. As your awareness of the systemic structure increases, you discover that your actions affect not only the people with whom you have direct contact, but also the people with whom *they* are in contact. Systems thinking confirms the old saying, "What goes around comes around." And according to internation-

13

ally known systems experts like Joseph M. Juran (1992) and W. Edwards Deming (1986), the systems structure creates between 85 and 94% of the problems in any organization.

It is obvious to those who work in schools that external forces (government, local communities, community members, parents, and students) attempt to manage them by control and mandate. But internal management forces, including the board of education, the superintendent, central administration, principal, teachers, and support employees also practice the same control and mandate style on a smaller scale. "Control and mandate" managers do not take the time to understand the systemic forces that work against them. Usually, they design controls for the "quick fix" of a problem that will recur, because its real cause is not addressed. They next seek to find a scapegoat, someone to blame. Of course, it is a waste of time to assign blame, if the system itself is responsible for the problem (Juran, 1992; Deming, 1986).

The "control and mandate" management style assumes that people will conform to management dictates. But we know that people sometimes ignore the chain of command, and that they often short-cut policies and procedures. In fact, the more control management exerts, the more it threatens personal visions. And the stronger the threat, the more people will try to protect their visions by resisting management.

Recently, when I lectured in a local school district, a member of the audience challenged my emphasis on the importance of systemic thinking. "If we do not control people they will do what they want and kids will not get educated," my critic argued. If the traditional control and mandate system of management worked, as this man insisted, our schools would have strong public support. But we know this is not the case. In *Thinking about Quality*, a book published in 1994, Lloyd Dobyns and Clare Crawford-Mason cited the National Commission of Excellence in Education report, "A Nation at Risk." The National Commission's report argues that U.S. students are not prepared to compete in the global workplace. Dobyns and Crawford-Mason state, "In the intervening ten years, public schools in the United States have gotten worse, not better" (p. 170). They claim, "For public education to improve, the system has to be changed from quantity to quality thinking,...no number of...legislative reforms will make it better" (p. 170). This is where the control and mandate management style has led our schools. If we must blame someone, we can blame everyone: government, communities, community members, parents, administrators, teachers, and employees. Together, we have created the system by which we educate our children. Collectively we are responsible for the past, but we have the power to change how we manage our schools.

If we want our schools to change, we cannot continue to do the same thing. We must change ourselves, not organizational charts, policies, and procedures, but how we develop and carry out policies and procedures. Insanity, a wise man once said, is doing the same thing and expecting different results. But that is what we have done with our schools. We control more, mandate more, blame more, shame more, and guilt more, trying to get different results. What has happened? We have created a predictable system described in national reports that tell the story of schools getting worse and worse.

WHAT CAN BE DONE?

Do not scrap the old system! The trick we must figure out is how to improve the system we have. Why? Because no matter how out of control the old system may be, how poorly it seems to function, how politically torn it is, parts of this system are stable and/or predictable. In addition, it is easier to identify system processes that are out of control when they are in operation. And most importantly, the people who work in the system can help to identify and work toward eliminating the root causes of problems. Their involvement in the process of correcting the system gives them the opportunity to change the pictures in their albums, their mental models, their visions.

Resist the temptation to solve school problems by creating a new system. Think about anything you have attempted to learn. For example, as you learned how to work with a computer, remember how frustrating it was to learn how to operate a spreadsheet program. Then only one year later, it did not meet your needs and you had to learn a new, more complex program. In learning the new spreadsheet program you discovered many of the same old commands so you learned and were productive more quickly. You used the parts of the old system that meet your needs and learned new skills to support current needs. Or, think about how you or a close friend felt when your physical needs required you to begin a new diet, low in sugar, salt, fat, or cholesterol. What diet practices were changed? You dropped only damaging amounts of one or more harmful ingredients. The remaining food practices were unchanged. In both cases, new learning and frustration occurred. New systems are difficult to accept! So, it is sensible to change only what needs changing.

Now think about all of the new problems you discovered during a change process. Usually, introducing a totally new system creates even more problems than you sought to correct! Eventually, of course, we learn how to cope or get past the problems created by the new system. Either we improve our techniques until our picture albums, mental models, paradigms, or visions correspond to the new system; or we revert to our old behaviors and use the old system. The point is, new systems also have problems. And new systems require making adjustments to our picture album, mental model, or vision, just as adjustments are required to keep the old system working.

Consider the energy required to change the total educational system. The change will, predictably, create a new set of problems. Wouldn't it be a better use of human and capital resources to improve the existing system? By giving people the chance to solve problems created by key patterns in the systemic structure, we also give them the opportunity to change their mental models.

What can be done? How can we improve the systemic processes that currently prevent schools from meeting or exceeding the public's expectations? We can achieve the necessary changes by combining systems thinking with the application of tools and principles that support continuous improvement.

When we continue to use the "control and mandate" model of management, we as a society deny the fact that other forces, forces beyond our control, affect our schools. It is easy to point the finger of blame. But this is also a sign of weakness. It takes courage, hard work, and perseverance to work within the current system to correct its defects. It requires courage to change a system's structure so it allows people to open their minds and use their talents to understand the natural progress of interrelated patterns of activities and processes. And it requires courage and hard work to learn how to manage only the key patterns so we have the time to improve the processes that currently strangle our schools.

These comments may seem simplistic, even insulting. But as systems thinking becomes part of your vision and as you learn more about key patterns, you may decide it takes acts of heroism to improve student learning.

CHAPTER 3

Building a Systemic Model

Organizational models, in the form of organizational charts, written policies, and local, state, and federal laws, are designed to guide people's actions. These structures help keep individuals and society organized and safe. Laws are for the orderly functioning of society. But as history demonstrates, when laws are overly restrictive, people will take action to achieve additional freedom. Obviously, societies must strike a balance between the control government can exert and the freedom individuals desire.

Local communities, organizations, and schools also must balance the needs and wishes of individuals and the well-being of the larger society. As school administrators and school board members know, local community members, parents, teachers, and students all scrutinize their actions. The degree to which individuals, communities, and school employees accept administrative and board decisions is determined by the visions of those affected by the decisions.

For example, communities commonly respond to the issue of school taxes. People may say, "I don't want to pay higher taxes," or "I am not against taxes to support the school, I just feel they are too high." What do these statements mean? Until we know more about the visions of the people who make such comments, we really know only that they are expressing a level of discontent with school taxes. Perhaps they simply can't afford to pay higher taxes. Perhaps they would be happy to pay higher taxes for a different kind of school. All we can do is speculate about the meaning of such comments. Only you could say specifically what *you* would mean by such a statement.

If you've made such comments, don't feel guilty! You are part of the system and you were honestly expressing your feelings. If you've been on the receiving end of these comments, don't take them personally! The comment may have nothing to do with you as board member, superintendent, or school employee. People who make such comments are reacting either to protect their visions of a good school or to answer personal issues outside the school's control. People may oppose tax increases because they and their community are suffering from the loss of industry and local jobs, widespread salary cuts, inflation, change in

17

the overall tax structure, or some other crisis. We don't know the real issue until we can study *why* people react in a particular way.

This is easier to say than to do. Schools are often forced into action on the basis of very few facts, offered up by only a few people. This is especially true when something negative happens to a child. (For now, I will leave it to you to define what "something negative" could be.) Parents storm the superintendent's office, the school board meeting, and/or the principal's office and demand action. If the parents have political power, they often can force action without real evidence of a need for change.

"SPECIAL CAUSE" AND "COMMON CAUSE" PERSPECTIVES

Before taking action to solve a problem, it is important to determine what kind of circumstances caused the problem. The case described above may be a "special cause" problem. Imagine that a school bus has gone into a ditch, and a child has been injured in the accident. The parents—or the entire community—may demand that the bus driver be fired. They may also insist the board take action against the transportation director or the superintendent for not properly supervising the driver.

At this point, the facts of the case are not completely known, and parents may be speculating about the cause of the accident. If these parents are politically powerful, they will be able to force punitive action on the driver and others in the system. But imagine that, after the board has acted, new facts come out: this was the first bus to go into a ditch in 3 years, and the driver was trying to avoid a collision with another vehicle. Or, this was the first bus accident in 20 years in which a student was injured. Consider the damage that has been done to the driver and other people involved in the incident because the community reacted to a "special cause" problem, an event that happened at random. We have little or no ability to prevent "special cause" problems.

"COMMON CAUSE" PROBLEMS

"Common cause" problems are predictable, but over time are accepted as the "way things are." They occur because of weaknesses in the system. Now imagine a community in which school bus accidents injure between one and three children each year. Minor accidents and skids happen every other week. In this community, parents and community members may become accustomed to the problem, because it happens with such regularity that people no longer think about it as unusual. It is no longer news, having become an accepted part of community life. (In an actual case, action was not taken until the school district's insurance company threatened to drop their policy.)

Notice the difference between the first bus accident case and the second. In the first case, parents demanded action to solve an unpredicted and unusual "special cause" problem. Making changes in the transportation system is unlikely to prevent the next accident (Juran, 1992; Deming, 1986). In the second case, few parents took action to solve a "common cause" problem. However, making changes in the transportation system is likely to reduce the number of accidents and injuries, but people did not perceive action was needed. It is likely that making changes in the transportation system will reduce the number of accidents and injuries (Juran, 1992; Deming, 1986). In both cases, parents based their reactions on their perceptions of the need for and likelihood of action. Their actions were controlled by their mental models. But in both cases, the visions led the community to act in error, without looking at the facts.

THE BALANCE MODEL (LILYQUIST, 1995)

Both cases illustrate the struggle to balance the need for a safe society with results produced by the school transportation system. In general terms, society seeks to maintain a reasonable balance between the needs of customers (students, parents, and the greater community) and those of the provider (the school system). In Fig. 3.1, customers are the external culture and providers are the internal culture. But in each example we see that the relationships between these groups are controlled by individuals' visions of a safe society, the pictures in their albums, their mental models, their paradigms.

Figure 3.1 illustrates the balance of forces in such situations. When one group (or culture) is unhappy with the results produced by another, there is an imbalance between visions and results. In Fig. 3.1, the visions of the external and internal cultures are in balance; therefore, neither culture is motivated to take any action. Current perception and vision are in balance.

Understanding Fig. 3.1 is the first step in systems thinking. The External Culture includes all people who are not part of and benefit from a particular process. For example, a school district's External Culture includes all stakeholders (customers): students, parents, community members, employers, and local, state, and federal governments. The Internal Culture is comprised of all people who are part of the process. The district's Internal Culture includes board

Figure 3.1. Balance model—external and internal cultures.

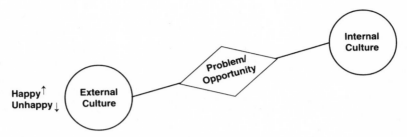

Figure 3.2. Imbalance—internal culture happy.

members, administrators, union leaders, informal leaders, teachers, educational assistants, secretaries, bookkeepers, cooks, janitors, bus drivers, and school volunteers.

On a smaller scale, the External Culture for a teacher's classroom includes the students, parents, community members, employers, and local, state, and federal governments, as well as school board members, administrators, union leaders, informal leaders, other teachers, educational assistants, secretaries, bookkeepers, cooks, janitors, bus drivers, and school volunteers.

Note that students are included in the External Culture for both school districts and teachers. As a consultant, I encounter questions by teachers, administrators, and some colleagues about whether students belong in the External or Internal Culture of a school. Chapter 6 explains why I place them in the External Culture as stakeholders.

Figure 3.1 appears to suggest that people must either win or lose when they react to a condition that threatens their vision. This is not the intent of the model, which simply points out a relationship between the actions people take and their vision of what should be (which may or may not be what is). This presents the opportunity for improvement that is gained by the identification and clarification of a problem, which may or does create an imbalance between the visions of the cultures.

Using Fig. 3.1, we can demonstrate the operation of balance and imbalance. First using a historic example, before 1215, the king (Internal Culture) dominated England and the people (External Culture) were unhappy (represented by the downward side of the balance in Fig. 3.2). The king provided a service, government, which affected people's lives. The people received both benefits and burdens of King John's decisions. In 1215, at the signing of the Magna Carta, the people were forcing the king to balance his actions with their beliefs, values, norms, and mores. This brought the system to a more balanced state, but left the king with less power and gave more rights to the people (Fig. 3.3). Figure 3.3 simply suggests that when major changes occur there may be a shift in how internal or external cultures perceive the result of change.

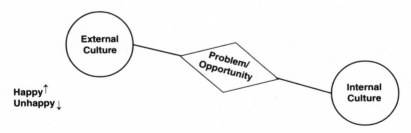

Figure 3.3. Imbalance—external culture happy.

The bus accidents can be analyzed in a similar manner. In the first case, parents (External Culture) were not happy because their vision of safe transportation was "accident-free." They reacted to an accident, forcing the school (Internal Culture) into action (Fig. 3.2). If the parents' action justifiably removed the driver and/or called the superintendent and transportation to account, Fig. 3.3 would show the changed balance.

In the second bus accident case, the vision of the parents and community was balanced by the results the transportation system produced. The system remained in balance (Fig. 3.1). In such a case, both the external and internal cultures do not take action. If change in the transportation system were instituted, parents' and community's or school district's current vision might not match the change. Then the scale would tip and reflect Fig. 3.2 or 3.3. Or, parents' and community's or school district's vision may be the same, resulting in a balance with both cultures unhappy or happy (Figs. 3.4 and 3.5). Until parents and community and school district commit to a position, the assumption is a balance between current perceptions and visions, as in Fig. 3.1.

From the perspective of a school, the ideal results exceed the visions of both the external and internal cultures. This situation is illustrated by Fig. 3.5. Alternatively, both want action, achieving results below the visions held by both the external and internal cultures. This situation is illustrated by Fig. 3.4. Because both cultures share the same vision, however, it is possible to argue that Figs. 3.4 and 3.5 do not differ from Fig. 3.1.

The fine points of Figs. 3.1, 3.4, and 3.5 are important to my argument. It is essential to remember that results produced by either the external or the internal culture will prompt a predictable response from the other culture. When the visions of the two cultures are significantly out of balance, people will take action on behalf of their own vision.

Systems thinking uses the systemic structure—a description of how people react to special and common cause problems—to analyze the relationships between external and internal cultures. It may help to think of the way the balance

Figure 3.4. Unhappy balance—both cultures.

of natural forces maintains our physical environment. In regions thought of as having hot and dry weather, we still find a range of temperatures and humidity. Even in hot, dry climates there are periods of unseasonable warmth and dryness. Over time, nature generally balances the system with unseasonably cold weather and rain.

Similarly, if we accept high levels of safe or unsafe conditions as normal, we react accordingly. Like the weather patterns that, over time, return a given environment to a predictable "normal" state, we react when conditions, or our perceptions of reality, do not match our vision of what is normal. Unfortunately, however, we may use our individual visions as the measure of all reality as it relates to schools.

Think of the problem of changes in student test scores. Slight variations in test scores at a high-achieving school may cause parents and community members to take action. For example, if one of 400 schools in a state moves from 10th to 15th in rank, the change is likely the result of common causes in variations of test scores. But a community accustomed to a high-ranking school may treat the drop in rank as a special cause and assume that "someone screwed up."

On the other hand, a community whose school always ranks near the middle may not be concerned even if the ranking changes up or down by 40 schools one way or the other. This community's vision of a good school is one with average test scores. The reality matches the community's beliefs, values, norms, and mores. And yet changing rank by 40 schools in one year is most likely

Figure 3.5. Happy balance—both cultures.

related to a special cause. Something has occurred to drastically change the test results. Perhaps the school changed the method of delivering instruction over a three year period, and should celebrate the success. Alternatively, in one year none of the special education students took the test. In either case, special action changed the test scores.

In the most tragic cases, schools that score at the bottom, the parents and community feel defeated and powerless to improve their schools. Low test scores are predictable and classified as a "common cause." The community makes no effort to change because they hold a vision that says "we cannot cause any change to improve our school." Parents might say, "The forces are too great to overcome." These parents are treating this common cause problem as a special cause problem by their lack of ability to act.

THE CONCEPT OF BALANCE

The balance model suggests that change will affect a person's vision. That is why the balance model is useful. If a special change occurs, or if common cause problems are recognized as out of control (far removed from the vision of either the external or internal culture), that culture is likely to oppose change or demand action. Two examples follow to help clarify special and common cause problems moving the balance model out of balance.

When conditions are extreme, people may demand action to address special cause problems; but the causes cannot be controlled. Conversely, people may not react at all to a common cause problem, because they have become accustomed to an extreme condition that matches their vision. The first example shows they are treating a common cause problem as a special cause problem, and assuming actions cannot solve it. The second example shows people treating a common cause problem as a special cause problem, even though actions can solve it. Both groups are acting in error.

According to Juran (1992) and Deming (1986) people should not waste their time on special cause problems. These consultants claim action will result in little or no gain. Rather people should take action to correct common cause problems. Applying Deming's and Juran's theory will guide the model into balance. In applying this theory, there does seem to be a band of tolerance within which change can occur without opposition (Lilyquist, 1995). Small incremental changes made over time allow people's visions to move toward the new condition.

The stranglehold on schools results from the ways people react to special cause and common cause problems. They respond to their vision rather than to facts, hard evidence that reasonable people agree on. Recall the classic line on the TV show *Dragnet*: "Please, ma'am, just the facts."

SUMMARY

The balance model describes two pieces of a systemic structure: the external and internal cultures. Both of these organizational dimensions refer to people and the beliefs, values, norms, and mores from which they develop their vision of a good school. We struggle for what we value, and we value what we have learned from our vision, our pictures in the album, our mental models.

What factors affect people's visions, and how do they react to these factors? The next chapter explains how people naturally respond to four additional dimensions of the systemic structure: leadership, strategies, structure, and results.

CHAPTER 4

Systemic Alignment and Balance

Do people protect their vision of a school? The alignment model suggests that people act along four dimensions: leadership, strategies, structure, and results. People use attributes of these four dimensions to control results that threaten or enhance their visions. As you read this chapter, which explains each dimension, judge the system rather than the individual actors. You will discover that the system itself teaches people how to react to the results the system produces! We will build this model as we look at the four dimensions and two cultures in this chapter. If you wish to look ahead, the complete model is presented in Fig. 4.6.

LEADERSHIP (FORMAL AND INFORMAL)

What is leadership? In Chapter 2, we discussed the control and mandate management style used by the formal leadership of many schools to control the results schools produce. Formal leadership positions are elected or appointed through processes determined by the organizational structure. Formal leadership includes the elected president, governor, local officials, and school board members, and their appointees, such as cabinet members, bureau directors, school superintendents, central office managers, principals, and teachers. Union leaders, negotiators, and others elected to govern school-related organizations are also formal leaders. Most people recognize formal leaders by their titles and by the actions they take to control and mandate compliance.

Informal leaders may not be so easy to recognize, but they are all around us. Informal leaders are people who are not elected or appointed, but who can influence decisions directly or indirectly. Decisions made by informal leadership can have as much power as the law within a particular culture.

Actions taken by formal leadership are intended to return the external and internal cultures to balance. Unfortunately, the leadership of the culture taking

Figure 4.1. Leadership formal/informal.

action may go beyond the balance point. This locks both cultures in a strangle-hold, with each attempting to gain the advantage to protect their vision of a good school/classroom. Although this concept is easy to grasp, it is useful to apply the theory of systemic structure to fully understand the interaction between formal and informal leadership.

Informal leadership exists in both external and internal cultures. To understand its influence on formal leadership, consider a sequence of snapshots in time, as informal leaders attempt either to control the formal leadership of their own culture, or to influence members of the other culture. In the external culture, informal leaders exert control to remove threats or to enhance their vision of a good school. In the internal culture, informal leaders exert control to remove threats or enhance their vision of a good school and/or a good classroom.

Imagine what happens when both the formal and informal leadership from both the external and internal cultures are working toward different visions simultaneously! Four leadership groups are attempting to remove threats, or to enhance at least four different visions of a good school! Every leadership group is working hard, but each is working to achieve a different vision. The leadership group's struggle is to control the structure to protect or enhance their vision. Observations suggest that the struggle over control by leadership groups creates barriers to improving the overall educational system. Simply, there is a lack of common vision of what schools are to achieve (Lilyquist, 1995).

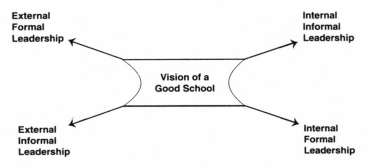

Figure 4.2. Leadership: competing visions of a good school.

The basic strategy used by informal leadership to protect its vision is to attack or remove the formal leader, create instability, or make the formal leader powerless (Lilyquist, 1995). A person with more than 20 years in a position of informal leadership once told me, "We had to make them leave because they were ruining our school." The person who made this comment was in charge of a program ranked in the bottom 10% in the state! What was this person protecting? A personal vision of a good program. This vision was not aligned with the state's expectations, but the local community found it acceptable.

In this case, the informal leadership's strategy created a win—lose situation based on gut feelings. Would the results have been different if informal leadership looked at the facts? We will never know for sure, but test scores that had been rising returned to their previous low levels after the formal leader was forced out (Lilyquist, 1995).

STRATEGY

Formal and informal leadership develop strategies designed to protect or enhance their visions of a good school. Strategies may be developed at macro or micro levels. At a macro level, the President's Conference on Schools in 1990 created a national strategy to improve schools; the resulting legislation was the Goals 2000: Education America Act (United States Congress, 1994). On a quite different (micro) level, purchase of a classroom computer might be a strategy developed to increase the use of technology in a school. Most strategies are designed to change the organizational structure, thereby changing the results the organization produces. However, there are two main sources of blockage inherent in a school's organizational structure. First, guidelines to develop strategies are often unclear or not followed. Second, schools frequently lack a common definition of their mission. (This factor alone blocks attempts to improve schools.) In addition, systems thinking suggests that other unexplained or unknown forces may block strategies.

Informal leadership may block attempts to carry out improvement strategies that threaten social rankings within the organization, block teachers' ability

Figure 4.3. Leadership, strategy.

to maintain their status through rewards, or threaten their vision. Informal leadership will first attack the formal leadership, but if they are unsuccessful in this, they will attack the improvement strategy.

For example, consider a school district that needs to restructure grade-level assignments within buildings because of financial circumstances or a shift in population. Resistance develops when people are moved to fill positions created by the change. In fact, this resistance could be predicted. Moving people from one building to another or shifting a grade level changes the social ranking within the district, changes individual teachers' ability to maintain their status, and threatens their visions of a good school or classroom.

Regarding this book, an editor raised the question, "Do formal leadership carry out any blockage strategies?" On a macro level, observations suggest that formal leaders take seriously the responsibility of carrying out laws and mandates from state and federal government, but they too have visions and mental models. On a micro level, formal leaders' action can block strategies by favoring powerful informal leadership structures to protect their position. In Chapter 8, interactions between formal and informal leadership are explained.

STRUCTURE

The structural dimension is defined as the combination of formal and informal interactions between and among people in the external and internal environments that influence administration, methods for improvement, conflict, instructional coordination, all services, and fixed assets. In simple terms, structure is everything that happens in a school district to produce results.

The systemic structure can—and does—block school improvement. If formal leaders succeed at developing and implementing a strategy for improvement, informal leadership can still block the strategy in two ways. First, informal

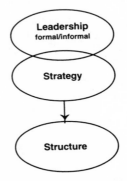

Figure 4.4. Leadership, strategy, structure.

leaders can simply say they are doing what they have been asked to do, but not do it. A more sophisticated and subtle version of this method of resistance involves reframing the strategy to match what is already being done. Second, informal leaders can bog down implementation of the strategy by making it more complex. Informal leadership may add steps to the strategy or set up an elaborate, dysfunctional committee structure that obscures the fact that the existing structure continues to control the organization and its operation.

The assumption may be that formal leaders do not block improvement strategies. In consulting work where I have explained this theory, I have found formal leaders do block change. What seemed to happen is formal leaders align themselves with the powerful informal leadership and work through or with them to block changes that they believe threaten both of their visions of a good school.

RESULTS

The external and internal cultures react to results, both real and perceived, produced by the school's organization. The reaction is caused by a culture's perception of whether the results threaten or enhance its vision of the school. Individuals and cultures are sensitive to how they are perceived by others. Their beliefs about the school are influenced by methods of monitoring student achievement, evaluating personnel, and using and misusing data. The results a school produces are thus subject to systemic structures influencing cultural beliefs, values, norms, and mores.

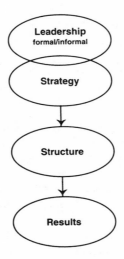

Figure 4.5. Leadership, strategy, structure, results.

Actions taken on the basis of the results dimension can and do try to block attempts to improve schools. For example, state leaders in Wisconsin developed a strategy—statewide testing of reading in the third grade—to help identify weakness in the educational structure. At the end of the first year of testing, the media used the data to rank all of the elementary schools on a state and local level. This practice by informal leadership threatened teachers, principals, and superintendents professionally and personally, and challenged their personal visions. Carrying out the test changed the structure, but the threat that the test results could be used to compare and sanction individuals prompted individual schools and school districts to design and implement strategies to counteract the structural change.

The most common strategy involved pretesting third graders early in the school year. Some students were given extra help so they would score well. Others, who were determined to be incapable of scoring well, were exempted from taking the test through special education rules. One school scheduled the test for a time when their students (who had low scores on other tests) were absent from school. Obviously, the test was not being used as designed: to improve instruction for all students. In fact, individual schools circumvented the purpose of the test, and the state's national test scores remained unchanged.

Wisconsin's formal educational leadership invested enormous amounts of time and energy in creating a third-grade testing strategy designed to change the organizational structure and improve results. In the end, however, students as a group did not perform any better than they had before the test was introduced. When a third-grade teacher said, "Ah, that test is meaningless," her comment appeared to have merit. Action was taken in schools so that test results would not impact negatively on the school or classroom teacher. The test results were questionable because some students' ability to take the test was restricted or enhanced.

ALIGNMENT AND BALANCE

The four dimensions we have been discussing—leadership, strategy, structure, and results—can be called "alignment dimensions," and each has a special relationship with the balance dimensions (external and internal cultures) we considered in the last chapter (Fig. 4.6). Leadership takes action to develop strategy that will change the structure and thereby change results, in order to bring about or maintain balance between the external and internal cultures. In each of the alignment dimensions, systemic forces from the balance dimensions can and do block school improvement. Thus, when action is planned in any one of the six dimensions, that dimension is influenced by the other five.

You can also think of the balance and alignment dimensions as "people" and "process" factors. People, of course, constitute the external and internal

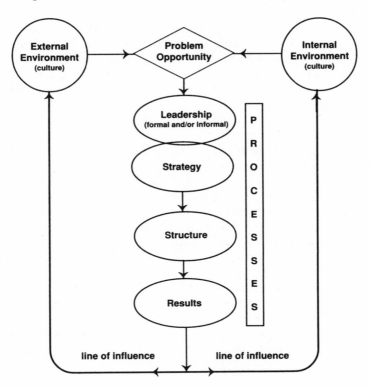

The model represents a system in a state of balance. The problems are resolved between the *External and Internal environment cultures;* therefore, the lines of influence connecting the "problem" to the *External and Internal environment cultures* are straight, representing balance. When the lines of influence connecting the results dimension to the *External and Internal environment cultures* changes, a problem is created, unbalancing the system. To return the system to a balanced state, the *leadership* and *strategy* dimensions interact, to change the *structure* dimension, to produce a difference in the *results* dimension, that changes the influence to balance the *External and Internal environment cultures* dimensions. This model is based on the work of Lilyquist (1995), Hmaidan (1991), Mohd Nor (1989), Stampen (1987), and Shirley & Caruters, (1979).

Figure 4.6. The balance alignment model.

environments or cultures. Processes—the alignment dimensions—require that people take action. If no action were ever taken, there would be no leadership, no strategies, no structure, no results. In fact, there would be no school system!

The interrelationship between all of these dimensions is complex, and the balance alignment model oversimplifies a systemic structure. It does, however, provide a visual model (Fig. 4.6) that helps in understanding systems thinking.

Figure 4.6 illustrates how lines of influence connect the balance and alignment dimensions. A common pattern of events flows through the six dimensions as the balance is in a continuous state of change.

Readers will find it useful to refer back to the balance alignment model as future chapters offer snapshots of factors that affect teachers' attitudes toward school improvement. The stories related in those chapters are accounts of actual events as recorded through interviews, observations, and a review of pertinent documents. Some of the stories will make you angry, but it is important not to blame the people in the stories. The system, acting in the way the balance alignment model illustrates, has taught these people what to do.

During the research for this book, I interviewed an elementary school teacher with more than 20 years of experience. I asked her why teachers focus on self-preservation rather than on improving student learning. She exclaimed, "I have never gotten a demand for improvement. I have gotten a demand for change." After I completed my formal research report, she wrote me a short note: "I obtained a copy ... through the public library and read it with interest and with some dismay. What a dreary little soap opera! The prospects for change do not seem bright. Perhaps we should strive for *improvements* instead."

This teacher has learned the most important lesson I hope my research will teach: Focus on the possibilities for improvement, not the negative demands of the past. ***Don't blame people. It is the system that creates most of the problems—and also the opportunities to improve.***

CHAPTER 5

Stakeholders I: Community, Community Members

INTRODUCTION

Current thinking suggests that ineffective schools will become effective if they carry out the best practices found in effective schools. In other words, mandating improvements will improve schools. However, combine the balance alignment model with the idea that peoples' visions determine whether or not they take action. This suggests that *mandating* changes will only increase the resistance to school improvement efforts! As seen in Chapter 3, communities react differently to special cause and common cause problems. Also, each community may have its own vision of good schools, and these may vary from place to place.

An angry teacher confronted me during a recent lecture. "What you are saying is top management should not control teachers. That's right, isn't it?" But that is not what I had said. This teacher had reframed the issue to conform with her vision.

What I meant was that announcing mandates and enforcing controls based on "gut feelings" may not do the job. To improve our schools, we need to take actions guided by a knowledge of organizational structure and theory. We can train people to make changes that are not self-destructive, but this will take heroic leadership, and will require people to learn systems thinking that leads to measurable improvement. We can find a better way than quick-fix mandates and controls imposed with no reliable measures of success.

COMMUNITY AS EXTERNAL ENVIRONMENT (CULTURE)

Each community has a unique way of reacting to the results its schools produce and has a different level of involvement in school activities. In one community,

33

school results may be perceived threats to its vision and activate a groundswell of activity. In another community, the same results may not threaten its vision, so that changes in results have little meaning and do not precipitate action.

I gave fictional names to the three communities studied by me, in order to help distinguish their unique characteristics. This chapter will introduce you to Dryden, Elkin, and Skyland so that you may develop an understanding and feeling about each community. In later chapters, as I introduce individuals and community members, you will be able to identify their hometowns by the first initial of their last name. In addition, a number is added denoting the order of introduction to the reader. Lori D1, for example, lives in Dryden and is the first person introduced in chapters 6 and 7.

Case Study One—Dryden

Dryden is located in a rural area of rolling hills, 40 miles from a medium-sized city and 60 miles from a major university. More than 50% of this region is in cultivation. Residents are employed in crop farming, or work in a few small local industries, or commute to the city for work. Most of the people who live in and around Dryden have long-time family ties to the area.

The school district has three school sites. The main site, located in Dryden, includes the district office, high school, middle school, and a fourth-through-sixth-grade elementary school. The other two sites are in very small towns less than 10 miles from the main site. They house elementary schools, one K–3 and the other K-4.

Stability. Dryden is very tolerant of school policy—until major issues challenge its vision. A two-term board member said, "Unfortunately, we don't get a lot of interest except for taxes, busing, and moving students." He was upset because after years of quiet, the board and the administration were under attack after restructuring grade levels at the elementary schools. This change in school structure resulted from spending controls imposed by the state legislature. Before the restructuring, each elementary school had a kindergarten to sixth-grade program. The restructuring, which caused some fourth-, fifth-, and sixth-grade students to be bused to Dryden, had reduced transportation costs and saved five of seven positions slated for layoffs.

Pressure. Dryden teachers report that comments and actions of community members, after the restructuring caused by cost controls, make them uncomfortable. Community members actions suggested that they believe the school structure would have remained if teachers received less pay or did more for no pay. A special education teacher who does not live in the district said, "The higher the power and status goes up, the more pressure we'll have. The public views teachers as having the summer off. The public does not understand that the teachers and the kids need a break." A 7-year teacher reported that his neighbors gave him a hard time about salaries and high pay raises. A husband and wife team reported that their friends said, "Look at all the big bucks they got." One teacher reported pressure from community athletic groups to spend more time at community activities. Teachers believe that high property taxes prompted the criticism of salaries. Teachers say they want to defend themselves, but usually say nothing to avoid making the situation worse.

Involvement. The school district routinely held public meetings before the restructuring, but only 30 to 50 people out of a population of 5000 were involved—until the board passed its motion to change the structure of the elementary schools. Then the community reacted with 200 people attending board meetings and bringing circulated petitions. A board member said he was concerned about the lack of community involvement before restructuring. "We need the community to define what is not acceptable," he said, "but they are not involved." According to a school aide who has lived in Dryden her entire life, "The community is not going to bother you if you don't make any fast changes. Big changes will cause problems." Even after the restructuring motion passed, only the parents and community members negatively affected by the changes were active in attempting to reinstate the kindergarten-to-sixth-grade structure. Community members who were not affected, and those who liked the change, continued to be inactive.

Restructuring moved some teachers from schools in which they had taught for 20 years, required some teachers to teach at different grade levels, and placed others in classrooms that were poorly organized for their style of teaching. However, some other teachers improved their social rank and had better rooms. Three powerful teachers were not moved. Teachers who changed school assignments were threatened by a loss of social standing. They lost the support of peers with whom they had worked for several years. One teacher said, "It was like losing one of your family. Three of us just sat down and cried."

On the one hand, teachers negatively affected by the changes attempted to organize the community to reinstate the original school structure. A teacher opposed to the change said, "We found out they [board of education and superintendent] listen, but they don't hear." Another teacher said, "The community is not persistent in [opposing] the change, so it went through." She believes that eventually the old structure will be reinstated. On the other hand, teachers whose social rank improved after the change, or who gained better teaching conditions, were observed to be working quietly to maintain the new structure.

The community's prior lack of involvement was evident in its lack of interest in school board elections. An office secretary recalled a successful write-in campaign for a school board nominee 15 years before. She said that after an issue related to the superintendent disappeared, the school did not hear from the community, until this restructuring.

A board member asserted that the three sites do not work well together. After one of the elementary schools was condemned, he related that the district had been forced to find classroom space in churches. The board tried three times without success to pass a bond referendum for a new school. Board members, aides, and teachers confirmed that the town that was to receive the new school voted for the bond issues, but the other two towns rejected them. Finally, a new state law was passed permitting school boards to borrow up to $1 million without a referendum, and the district built an addition to replace the condemned building.

Laura D1 who had taught in one of the churches, described a cold, dreary classroom removed from other teachers. She tried to get the bond issue passed by being active in the community. When the bond referendum failed, she blamed other teachers for not being involved.

Several events—the elementary school condemnation, failed bond referendums, borrowing of $1 million, and the state mandate restricting expenditures—forced the school district to restructure. Both the board and the superintendent came under attack. In response, the board backed away from a strong position of support for restructuring action. Teachers interpreted this to mean that the superintendent and the administrative staff had lost their ability to manage the district, and they blocked administrative actions that would solve problems caused by the restructuring. Unrest among the teaching staff persisted, and teachers continued to attack the administration as they sought to gain back what they had lost or to protect what was gained in the restructuring.

Comment. The sociological term (McCarty and Ramsey, 1968) for the Dryden community's political structure is "inert-latent." In such a structure, community members do not take action unless they perceive an extreme threat to their values, beliefs, norms, and mores. When there is an overwhelming threat to their vision, their latent interest lets them take action until they resolve the issue to their satisfaction; then the community will return to a state of rest or inertia until challenged again. In Dryden, community members and teachers were active when their vision was challenged, but usually they were uninvolved in school politics.

Dryden provides a good example of the "stranglehold" in action. Community members did not consider the welfare of the school district as a whole. Everyone agreed that a new building was needed, but community rivalries caused three referendums to fail. Similarly, community members liked the fact that school spending was being controlled; however, the consequences of controlling spending divided the community. The split caused people to expend energy protecting their visions of a good school. Dryden never collected data on whether—or how—the restructuring affected student learning. Such important questions were left to hearsay and gut feelings.

Case Study Two—Elkin

Elkin is located between two medium-sized cities, close to the interstate highway system. This is a rural community with large crop and dairy farms and some light industry. Residents are employed in local industries, business, and farming, or travel outside the community for employment. New residents are moving into Elkin, but the community is dominated by old family names and businesses. A teacher described the community by saying, "This community has small-town values. [They are] hard workers, [they] like to see people work, [they are] resistant to changes that are not proven. Some people are sixth generation in [the county]." The school district has four sites located in Elkin. One complex of buildings includes the district office, high school, and middle school. The other sites are elementary schools, kindergarten through fifth grade, distributed within the boundaries of the city.

Stability. The community is controlled by a few long-term residents. The superintendent, an elementary principal, a secretary, and teachers called these the "old guard." Observations and media reports suggest that the community is divided in its perceptions of the schools, but the "old guard" controls the district. According to the superintendent, the district started to change 15 years ago when third- and fourth-generation businesses were first sold to large corporations. He said, "Individually, they [the former business owners] controlled the economics of the town. They were 'old money'.... The old guard still controls things; however, 10 years ago they could start and stop anything in 10 minutes. Now it takes them a few days, but they can still stop projects from happening."

The community as a whole seems to accept the power of these informal leaders to control all aspects of the community. An office secretary (who was born and raised in the school district and had worked in the school for more than 20 years) asked me what I thought about the town and school. I answered, "This school is about as Middle America as you can get." "It is," she said, "and we plan to keep it that way."

She added, "We have executives [upper management at the corporations] that are making a six-figure income. We know that, but it's like we don't want to see.... The community does not accept new families. They want things to remain the same even though the community has changed." It appeared that by not recognizing her community had changed, she could maintain her beliefs about Elkin.

A teacher from Elkin said, "The community is friendly; everybody thinks they know what's going on with everyone. There are people [long-term community members] that have their set ideas and you cannot convince them of anything else."

The community has several restaurants. According to teachers, support staff, and administrators, the "old guard" eats breakfast and lunch at one of the restaurants, at a table with a "reserved" sign. Observation of the conversations among the men at this table suggested that they do control the town. The men discussed town politics, which businesses were doing well, and what should be changed. They never invited anyone else to join them, even when the restaurant was full and their table had an empty seat.

Pressure. Teachers held similar views about community pressure directed toward the school and employees. A teacher with 25 years of service in Elkin said, "Like the majority of taxpayers, they believe you have 3 months off, vacation during the year, and I agree, but I told them that is not why I did that [worked as a teacher]." She added, "I tell parents, if you like that [time off] you should look at going back to school and doing it." Observations suggest this teacher enjoys teaching and that having summers off is not her primary reason for being a teacher.

Teachers reported that 5 years ago, during contract negotiations, the community pressured the board not to raise salaries. The teachers reacted by planning and carrying out a work slowdown. One teacher recalled, "They would not give us the raise we wanted and we were trying to show what we did do." The community remains upset about the slowdown. A newly elected board member commented, "People don't accept teachers as not taking tickets, doing pompoms, or coaching. They look at that as 'those damn teachers.'" Other teachers commented on community expectations that teachers will participate in all school activities, before, during, and after school hours, with or without pay.

Teachers and administrators have different views of community support for bond issues (that is, capital investments for buildings). Teachers perceive the community as not supportive. A teacher argued, "People that have children in the school are positive and look out for the school. The people [who] don't, senior citizens, seem to find the negative things in the school district. Parents are supportive of a new school. Senior citizens don't see a need and believe the buildings we have are sufficient. Their solution is to have bigger classes and deal with it." Administrators think the community will support good schools. The superintendent said, "The community wants good education and is willing to pay for it. When they do things they do it right, top-of-the-line excellent buildings." Observations of old and new buildings confirm the superintendent's opinion.

Involvement. A select few members of the community are actively involved with the schools. Involved community members and parents can be found in the schools on most days. This was surprising because, during the period I was collecting information, the local newspaper regularly published negative articles about the school district. The intense involvement of a few people has caused the district to struggle over adding and dropping programs, use of textbooks, hands-on instruction, whole group and whole language issues, and the strategic plan. (A classroom of students receive instruction and work together as a class or in groups where ability of the members is not considered. All communication skills are taught and reinforced at the same time.) A teacher's comment clarified the nature of community involvement: "We have watchdogs. If we are too innovative, we get squelched."

Comment. The sociological term (McCarty and Ramsey, 1968) for describing Elkin's political structure is "monolithic-elitist." This mean that a single elite group controls the community: schools, the town government that provide services, and also the wealth and social structure of the community. This monolithic-elitist group stays in constant control.

Elkin, too, provides a good example of the stranglehold in action. In a monolithic-elitist power structure, it is difficult to make any change without the approval of the elitist group. This prevents any radical change from occurring. This may be good, but it also prevents new thinking from becoming part of the culture. The elitist group will prevent a business, groups of people, or individuals from becoming an integral part of the community unless they support the prevailing vision of the schools and the community's values. Most teachers stand silently on the fringe of power and claim they cannot attempt anything new. A few teachers are aligned with the community power structure and use their influence to protect or enhance their vision.

Case Study Three—Skyland

Skyland is a community that is changing from rural to suburban. It is located a short distance from a medium-sized city with a major university. The population is employed in farming and local light industry, or commutes to the metropolitan area. The population is split into two distinct groups. One consists primarily of blue-collar workers from families who are old-timers in the community. These people own most of the land and believe in good, but basic, education. They support slow change. They want their children to have the basic skills necessary to enter the work force, attend vocational college, or enter a university. Members of the other group are considered newcomers by the established population. Most have moved to Skyland in the last 10 years; they are professional people, including high-level government employees, professors, and business executives who commute to the city. They want good schools, defined by high technology and innovative educational programs; they want their children to be admitted to major universities.

The school district has three sites. The largest contains the district offices, high school, middle school, and a kindergarten-to-fifth-grade elementary school. Two additional kindergarten-to-fifth-grade elementary schools are located on separate sites, one in Skyland and the other on the edge of the nearby metropolitan community.

Stability. Skyland is locked in a political struggle between the two opposing groups. The local and metropolitan newspapers cover the community's discontent by conducting in-depth interviews with individuals from the opposing sides and comparing the comments. This practice has fueled the divisions within the community. A new factor has affected Skyland, the results of the recent school board election, where three conservative candidates narrowly unseated three liberal board members. The major dispute began when the district started to implement a strategic plan that had been developed by more than 350 people from the community. Observation, interviews, and review of documents support that long-time community members viewed the plan as a move away from basic education. New community members supported the plan, which included bold statements giving teachers broad latitude to carry out innovations.

Teachers share the belief that the community is changing, but they disagree about the causes and benefits of the change. A teacher born and raised in the district said, "It is getting to be a changing community. They move here because we have the greatest school system on earth. Give me a break, we are having trouble keeping the image up. It's hard for the older people and farmers because the taxes are getting too high for them. I feel we have lost the small-town feeling. Everyone is rushing off to [the nearby city] for their jobs. Most work in [the nearby city]." A teacher married to a person from the community said, "It was a farming community and is still some of that. [Skyland] is becoming a suburb of [the nearby city]. People commute to work.... We are middle class, white. We don't have many ethnic groups." A teacher with 20 years in the district said, "[Skyland] was a very middle-class white community. Now it is becoming very diverse because of the low-income housing and more blacks and other ethnic groups, Asians. These students are now bringing in their own culture. For...students that is threatening.... Things are changing and people are not willing to admit it." Another 20-year veteran said, "They are very well educated, middle class moving toward an urban from a small-town community. They are concerned about education."

Other aspects of the community are also changing. The superintendent reported having difficulty locating a new school in a rapidly developing area of the school district. He said, "I have had to fight about putting a school in a neighborhood. The residents are concerned because of the problems they are having in [the nearby city]." A teacher described this part of the district: "You have a set of parents that want their children to excel...and then the poor students try to meld.... There is a wide spectrum of economic backgrounds. We have a wide variation in the classes in town.... The district could not pay me enough to work in the...school [in that part of Skyland]."

Teachers talked about the "mental model" of the community, which differs from the teachers' perception of reality. According to one teacher, "The mental model of the parents is dad works outside the home and mom is in the home taking care of the kids." However, most teachers reported that in most homes mom and dad worked outside of the home. Another teacher said, "They want values to be taught around the kitchen table, but that is not how families operate. It is not the way it works. It used to be that children were in Scouts, church activities, and school. Now parents are chauffeurs." The conservative board and community members believed values should be, and were, taught around the kitchen table; they did not want the school teaching values. Liberal board and community members wanted children exposed to a wide range of cultures and values in school and believed children were not taught values in the home.

Observations suggested that the community was changing, despite resistance. In a restaurant, a group of older community members debated whether to sign a petition to block rezoning. One man said, "We don't need any more restaurants or motels." All of the people at the table signed the petition. In another restaurant, a group of women and men complained about construction on the highway connecting the metropolitan area to the town. A man said, "That highway would have been good enough for 10 more years." The rezoning was not blocked, and the new highway was developed.

Pressure. When teachers were asked to talk about Skyland they focused on community involvement in the school. One teacher said, "Our community is not backing the teachers. Last spring the paper made it sound like we were not doing our jobs. We as teachers made it worse than it was, but it is hard to separate yourself from the emotion." Another teacher said, "Once the paper sets the agenda, teachers would not be able to explain the whys and hows they would work toward improvements."

Two teachers were observed commenting on a news article about a principal. One teacher said, "It was not well-written.... Everything was taken out of context. The article was not fair." The other teacher asked, "What purpose did it serve?" Teachers called community support or involvement "pressure" from the community.

Involvement. During interviews, teachers primarily wanted to talk about community involvement in the schools, both positive and negative. A teacher who supported the recently elected conservative board members minimized the effects of the election, but other teachers were concerned that conservatives would control the new members. One teacher, Sam S1, refused to talk about either the election or the new board members. Observations and interviews suggested that she uses both old and new board members to control the decision-making process. (Her influence is explained in Chapter 7.)

A teacher who supports the newly elected conservative board members was asked, "How has the community affected your school?" She responded, "Apparently quite well. The community is supportive of the school. There are always a couple of negatives. I have a friend who is a realtor in [town]. She has people who want to be in the [Skyland] school district." I asked, "What impact have the news articles had on the school?" She said, "I take some of this stuff with a grain of salt. This is not the first time something like this happened. The paper really does not affect me. I don't pay much attention to the paper." The researcher observed the current issues of two local papers, *The [Nearby] Times* and the *State Journal*, on her desk. She carried a daily paper with her each morning when she arrived at school. Two other teachers, who were reported to be supportive of the new board members, turned down opportunities to be interviewed.

Other teachers reported a variety of concerns with the conservative group and its agenda. Teachers did not agree on the size of the group. One classroom teacher said, "This group is not more than 5% of the population...the reality is 1% or less." A teacher who teaches a split grade (half the children at one grade level and the other half, one full grade higher) said, "They're a small vocal group of the community, no more than 10%, maybe not that much. They are well-organized." Another teacher thinks this group is creating a bandwagon effect. She said, "I would like to see it stopped."

Teachers believe that the agenda of the conservative group affects them in different ways. A teacher with more than 15 years in the district said, "Part of the problem is the battle in this community of conservative old school and the current administration wants to go in another direction to stay in the forefront." Another teacher claimed, "They are trying to pit the teachers against the administration." A teacher active in district committee work said, "They do not want site-based management, they do not want schools doing their own thing. It is a power issue. They want teachers to be more responsive to their ways, and now it is money. The community wants top-down management."

A teacher said, "I question what their agenda really is. We have had a board member come and address the committee [about strategic planning]. They do not use a style of communication skills we want our children to learn or communicate with. They are threatening, name-calling." He suggested that "better information will be gotten from the truck stop." Another teacher said, "I heard the hidden agenda was they did not want equal opportunity for all students. They want to keep the minorities out of the community. After experience on the council, I think that is their agenda. I think it is frightening." She reported that a board member said, "We should not appreciate other cultures. We should be homogeneous."

Other teachers reported additional concerns: "The board members are focused on the test scores. That is primary to them regardless [of] if the child retains the information." "You have to be careful so you're not teaching one way of thinking. If you don't, they think you are trying to tell students how to think." "Last year was a rough year.... The multiage grades were being questioned. This became very political." "I cannot prove this, but these people are self-serving with their agenda. I believe it could be interpreted as fear that the lower-socio-economic-class people might take the slots away from their children; therefore, the lower group would get some of the spots at Harvard and other big universities. How we would improve the school will increase the eligibility of all children."

Board members indicated that the election was competitive and close, with the conservative candidates winning three seats. A new board member said, "We have a wide base of support. The last election showed that. The feeling in the community is, if it is not broken don't fix it." He explained that the community thinks it has had, and continues to have, a good educational system. The school has always scored high on standardized tests. He said, "We believed what was happening was going to dismantle a perfectly good system." He was asked whether he represented a minority or majority in the community. "I would not say the minority; on the contrary. We have a percentage, 10% to 20%, that understand the issue and the rest of the people are apathetic or don't care. There is some percentage on the other end. Under normal circumstances it is difficult to unseat incumbents and go against the changes. There has to be a good solid reason for bucking the system. We were able to generate more support than the current administration." Another new board member said, "I am concerned that someone [conservative group members] will have to pick up the pieces from all of the restructuring."

A board member who opposes the conservatives said, "I believe it has to do with having people make the adjustments in their mental model. People have all gone to a place called 'school.' The real question is why don't people move to the world news? [That is, why don't people work at having a world-view?] In this country there is a conventional look.... New curriculum is being challenged by the mainstream, the Harvard group. The Harvard group is the people who believe the new curriculum would prevent their children from going to the Ivy League college. [They believe] the...school's changes would not provide their children with an education that would help the children score high on entrance exams." This board member raised a question: "Why are we at where we're at? It is the same place. Nothing has really changed. The election caused everything to be put on hold or moved back toward where the school had come [from]."

Despite the community divisions, a bond issue passed easily. An educational assistant said, "If the community sees the need, we don't have a problem." A teacher with more than 20 years in the district confirmed the educational assistant's comments: "The community wants good schools and wants good buildings. They have supported bonds for buildings."

Comment. Skyland's political structure is called "factional-competitive." Skyland offers the simplest example of this sociological type, which includes at least two groups struggling to gain power over one another.

Skyland provides a case in which the formal and informal leadership of both the external and internal cultures are at odds. Two coalitions have formed: "back to basics" and "innovative instruction." Each is afraid that the school's educational program will not meet *their* vision. One group fears that implementing changes will result in their children being unprepared. The other group fears that if changes are *not* implemented, their children will not be prepared. So far, the conservatives have blocked the changes.

Both groups base their arguments on "gut feelings." If test scores support their position, they are cited. If test scores do not support their position, they claim the scores are not a good measure. Both groups are reacting to their visions of a good school. Both groups perceive change as a threat, but perceive it from opposing views.

SUMMARY

The cases of Dryden, Elkin, and Skyland confirm that different individuals can have quite different visions of a good school. Many factors must enter into systems thinking in an attempt to understand people's reaction to changes in the schools. The three types of communities described provide a basis for studying and understanding additional factors that cause people to react conservatively to suggestions for school improvement. In each community, individuals react to the results schools produce (or are attempting to produce), as compared to their individual visions of a good school.

In addition to the three types represented by Dryden, Elkin, and Skyland, McCarty and Ramsey (1968) discovered and explained a fourth type of political structure, "pluralistic-rational." In such a community, there is an even distribution of power among the residents, and data are valued in making decisions. Usually, different groups control different aspects of the community: the schools, town government, community housing, and so forth. A wide range of residents in these communities share common opinions, and people are easily accepted into the community. This type of community has not been studied from the perspective described in Chapter 1.

COMPARISON OF THE COMMUNITIES' POLITICAL POWER STRUCTURE

Each of the communities studied has a different tolerance to change. Dryden's inert-latent residents do not take action until a major change threatens their vision. When the vision is threatened, the community appears to unite around the common threat. Elkin's monolithic-elitist residents are always on guard to protect the stability of the schools and the community. The "old guard" will not allow any changes to occur that would threaten the political, social, or economic structure of the community. When the vision is threatened, the powerful few take action, and the threat is contained. Skyland's factional-competitive residents are locked in a struggle generated by a changing community, in which two opposing forces are struggling to gain competitive advantage. There is a movement to change the structure of the schools, and another to keep the structure the same. Both groups use the media and the political and social structure to mitigate the threat from the other side. *In each community, residents say they want good education, but the communities do not share a common definition, and the residents within each community do not share a common understanding of what a good school is.*

COMMUNITY VISIONS

Although each of the three communities has a different power structure, each community's relationship with its school seems to be based on a common principle. If a community perceives that a school is moving away from its vision of a good school, the community will act to return the school to the community vision. The actions that communities take affect teachers individually and collectively, when the community's vision differs from the teachers' vision.

The exact relationship between the specific actions a community takes and its vision of a good school is not clear from this study. In each case, the community attempted to maintain both the stability of its power structure and its vision of a good school.

In each district, conflict over change has caused community unrest. A community has taken action when it has perceived the school to be outside its vision. The communities differ on their degrees of tolerance, that is, the size of the gap between accepting the change and the community's willingness to take action. For example, Dryden's residents have a high tolerance for curriculum changes and a low tolerance for changing the school structure. Elkin's community has minimal tolerance for any change that is not accepted by the powerful few. Skyland's community has a high degree of tolerance, until it finally takes action. Then actions taken in this community appear intense compared to those in the other two cases. All cases suggest that communities are rigid and do not change easily.

Because communities tend to be rigid, when schools do change, teachers place themselves and their visions at risk. Their efforts to improve educational programs may be thwarted. In addition, community criticism of teachers increases when conditions of employment and educational costs exceed the community's willingness to pay. Both of these factors cause teachers to focus their efforts on maintaining stability in the educational program.

Some teachers in each district appear to be highly sensitive to community members' negative comments about working conditions and school expenditures. There are differences among these individuals, but the data suggest that some teachers place a higher priority than others on protecting themselves from public criticism. The community thus appears to have a stabilizing effect on teachers, promoting resistance to change.

In subsequent chapters, understanding the way the political power structure defines each community will help guide the reader through the discussion of other organizational dimensions of the school systems in each district. Chapter 6 completes the discussion of the external environment by looking at the effects of parents, students, and state and national governments on teachers.

CHAPTER 6

Stakeholders II: Parents, Students, and State and National Government

INTRODUCTION

The current body of knowledge to improve schools suggests that effective schools have a high degree of parent involvement in the school. Some communities appear to believe that having parent involvement in school may block school improvements meant to help all students. In each school studied, evidence suggested a lack of a common vision of a good school/classroom between parents and teachers, and among teachers. Teachers and parents seemed at odds as to what is good for student learning; therefore, teachers and parents remain in a "gut-wrenching" struggle to improve student learning (Lilyquist, 1995). The question is, "Does parent involvement in school impact student learning?" The information presented here suggests "yes." However, teachers' opinion of positive or negative effects depends on their vision of good classrooms.

PARENTAL CONTROL AND INVOLVEMENT

Teachers realize that parents have the potential to support or to sanction them, by influencing others inside and outside the school. This sets the stage for teachers to focus on issues of self-preservation.

In Dryden, parent involvement was minimal, but the few involved parents were positive and supportive. Even so, teachers used social time to discuss the negative effect parents could have on them.

In Elkin, teachers were divided in their feelings toward a small group of parents, who seemed to be used by other teachers and an administrator to control school activities. Teachers in the "in-group" were positive about parent involve-ment. Teachers outside the "in-group" perceived the parents as controlling.

In Skyland, the parents and teachers were split between two groups: those who supported the recent changes and those who were against them.

In all three schools, teachers feared individual parents who criticized them personally or professionally. All teachers indicated their recognition, by verbal statement or observed action, that protecting their vision of a classroom was dependent on parents, as were their reputations and treatment as professional educators.

Although such information is not conclusive, the parents' degree of activity in each school appears to mirror the community's power structure. In Dryden, neither parents nor community members were generally involved with the school. A few parents are involved in Elkin and attempted to control it; similarly, a few individuals controlled the community. In Skyland, both the parents and the community were divided in their support of changes the school had implemented, suggesting that parents' influence reached beyond the school and into the community.

Dryden

In Dryden, teachers as a group have ambivalent views on parent control and involvement. They believe that supportive parents help them to provide an instructional program, but they are concerned about a few parents who threaten their control over planned activities. Lori D1, a kindergarten teacher, reported a story about a mother who verbally attacked a teacher regarding a field trip. She said, "We had a parent telling us the zoo trip is not as educational as a roller skating party." The field trip to the zoo occurred, but the teachers spent time discussing how this decision may affect them in the future. As I investigated why teachers were so concerned, I discovered a prior event had taught them to be concerned.

A year earlier, the parent of a special education student single-handedly caused the district to change the early childhood program and transportation routes. When discussing the change, a 12-year board member said, "She went to [the president of the board] a lot. [Connie D] can do that. She volunteered and was involved with school. ... I have a tendency to listen more to the people who constantly talk to me ." He explained that the board did not take action; they told the administration to take care of extending the early childhood program.

An educational assistant said, "We have only five parents who are in-volved. The other parents only come for conferences and programs." Still, teachers reacted to parent involvement as control. Teachers believe that parents do communicate with other parents. Lori D1 said, "As long as information to other parents is correct, you can use it to your advantage." Later she said, "I don't think parents have as much control as they used to; the [superintendent/principal] is putting [the child's problem] back in their lap. They cannot put the blame [for the child's problems] on the teacher." A teacher who was afraid she would receive a child with controlling parents explained, "I like what I do, parents have too much control." Then she contradicted herself: "I don't think parents participate in the child's learning. Parents in this district don't understand how important that is."

In sharp contrast to three classroom teachers, a special education teacher had this opinion. "If I didn't have the parents I would be sunk. I have to have them on my side. I have yet to not have a parent help me. They have to feel I am not a threat to them."

Elkin

Teachers' perception of parents' involvement depended on whether they were members of the "in-group" or "out-group." The in-group seemed to have power to control a parent's action to support or enhance the teacher's vision of a good classroom. Teachers in the out-group seemed to have little power and were forced to conform to the in-group's vision of a good classroom. An elementary teacher said, "You would have to talk to people that work here. They like it, or they are miserable about it." Kathy E1, a teacher with 25 years' experience, said, "Think of [parents] as allies until they prove otherwise."

Kathy E1 had a support group of 10 to 15 parents, whom she controlled. They were successful at blocking budget cuts, which could change Kathy E1's control of her classroom, by speaking at district and school budget hearings. On a daily basis four or five influential parents volunteered work in the school, which Kathy E1 encouraged. She used these contacts to promote her vision of a good classroom. Teachers closely aligned with Kathy E1 were pleased with the parents' actions.

At the same time, teachers and parents were split over a proposal not to purchase language arts textbooks, and use the money to purchase customized, self-developed materials for instruction. The administration agreed with the teachers, not to purchase textbooks, which caused conservative parents and traditional teachers to pressure both the board and the administration. One teacher explained, "They wanted a textbook so the parents could help the children at home." A teacher who did not want the textbooks said, "The parents put pressure on the administration and board to say you [teachers] will select the book." The parents and teachers wanting the change pressured the building principal. A teacher said, "The teachers argued that they were professional and could teach without a textbook." In the end, both groups perceived that they had won. The district purchased a new set of textbooks and permitted individual teachers to use the methods and materials they believed were the best for teaching language skills. What was interesting is Kathy E1 never wanted the change to happen.

At the building level, teachers view parent involvement differently. Teachers are divided about whether (5 to 10) parents should continue to control Good Behavior Day, Family Night, money for self-selected field trips, purchase of equipment for specific teachers, and the content of student programs. One teacher concerned about parental control said, "The president of the PTO [Parent–Teacher–Organization] said to [the principal], 'Don't ask her what she wants, tell her what to do.'" The principal required the teacher to change the program.

Teachers who were not closely aligned with Kathy E1's group of parents and teachers, "do not like how parents control the school." When interviewing teachers, it was interesting to note they were unaware that Kathy E1 controlled what occurred in the school. Teachers in the out-group blamed the parents for being too controlling.

Skyland

Teachers in Skyland were concerned over the current community climate focused on setting school policies. The recent campaigns for school board election clearly established there were two general visions of a good school district held by community members and parents. Teachers were split along similar lines. Some teachers' vision of a good classroom meant the use of traditional teaching methods; a basic curriculum in reading, writing, math, and science; and excluding the teaching of values in social studies. Others teachers' vision supported innovative teaching methods and additions to the traditional curriculum, such as computers, multimedia, and open discussion on values and social behaviors. Teachers' concern about parent involvement was based on their perception of how parents would change, maintain, or enhance their vision of a good classroom.

The superintendent said, "It is clear we have parents with concerns that affect how teachers teach. It does vary with teachers." Teachers say they do react to pressure from parents. One teacher explained, "I had the idea I could do anything I desired to do in my classroom. Now when I teach art from the Middle Ages or medieval times, I am concerned that the parents will claim I am teaching religion, because the Catholic Church funded most of the art." Later in the interview the teacher said, "Because of the [school board] election I am always questioning myself. I am afraid of the change and facing criticism. Now I am more cautious...I rehearse everything I am going to say...I am protecting myself, because I don't know what will happen." A teacher reported, "You have parents coming into your room inspecting worksheets, letters, and homework, questioning everything you do. I didn't have it happen to me, but it did to the person across the hall." The principal and other teachers confirmed the story with actual dates and events; although the teacher denied parents came to her room, she was observed regularly seeking support for action she took in her classroom. Another teacher said, "There was tension all year."

Four teachers in the school had children of critical conservative parents in their rooms. One said, "She [the child's mother] questioned how do you teach and what do you teach. She was very nice." Another teacher said, "So far the parent has been supportive." One teacher refused to be interviewed; others said she had a negative experience with conservative parents. A fourth teacher agreed to an interview, but insisted, "You cannot write any of this." One teacher said, "We should not have them coming into our classrooms and telling us how to do...."

If parents are involved and supportive of the teachers, teachers view them as allies and want them to become more involved. A teacher with more than 20 years in the district, who was aligned with the conservative community, said, "They [parents] are supportive and want their children to do well, but [they] don't put a lot of pressure on the teachers. Parents are willing to volunteer and help with homework, but don't come in on demand. If they want something they do it nicely." A teacher with experience in other schools said, "Parents are appreciative here. In other schools they applied a lot more pressure.... [Teachers here] would do anything you asked of them." Another teacher added, "Those parents that are active in the school and know what is going on are a good thing [parents support my position]."

Sam S1 is a teacher who would not talk about her relationships with parents or with the new conservative board members, but was observed meeting with the PTO's president and talking about what was happening at another elementary school in the district. Summing up parent involvement this teacher said, "I think the education in [town] has always been good and we needed to keep up and have families more involved.... Families need to feel comfortable about the school."

Later it was found Sam S1 had described her math program as back-to-basics for the conservatives, and as innovative to advocates of change. Parents and teachers from both factions thought of Sam S1 as a good teacher. Sam S1 taught math in some form, for all subject areas during the whole school day. Everything she did was related to numbers or calculations. Observations suggest that reading, spelling, science, social studies, and any other required subjects were secondary; however, Sam S1's teaching style supported the liberal vision of a good classroom, reflecting her innovative approach of instruction.

What best described teachers' feeling regarding parent involvement was fear. Fear controlled the action of teachers, and fear caused them to be cautious of carrying out any change. Teachers did not know whose vision of a good school was safe to work toward, so the safest vision was within their classroom. There they have learned how to protect their vision of good education and protect themselves from external forces.

Skyland presents an extreme case of parents' effects on teachers. In all schools, teachers want parent involvement when it enhances their vision of a good school or classroom, and are threatened when it is contrary.

Each case suggests that teachers are aware of the political pressure parents can apply. The next chapters will explain why and how teachers use or mitigate political power. It is important to refer to the Balance Model, when analyzing why and how teachers or parents and community members take action. Again, do not judge actions taken by people; they are protecting or enhancing their vision of a good classroom/school.

PARENTS: TEACHER-BLAMING

Teachers seem to fear being blamed by parents for errors they made or being blamed for issues outside the teachers control. The flip side of being blamed by parents is parents not acting to help their child. Teachers' fears are based on personal stories or observing the effects parent have had on other teachers. Bonnie D, a Dryden second-grade teacher, told about a parent who called her at home while drinking to complain that she had made a mistake in grading a paper. She asked to have the paper returned. Even after she apologized for an error and agreed to change the grade, the parent continued to complain—for more than 10 years. The teacher is still concerned about the parent talking to others in the community. She concluded her comments by saying, "I have had three parents that were not supportive. Not bad for 30 years of teaching."

Lori D1 was blamed for a child's problems in school. The guardian claimed that if the child had gone to preschool, he would be okay. The teacher said she responded, "You had him for 4 years. If you would have worked with him he would have been OK. I turned it back on her. Parents need to be responsible for that early learning."

An Elkin third-grade teacher said, "Parents have their own ideas on how the child should be taught. If you're not teaching what they want, they can be a threat." She explained that 2 years ago, a father sent the principal a letter citing concerns about her teaching and blaming her because his child was not learning. She claimed that the father had never been in her classroom and the child lived with the mother. The principal supported her teaching, but in the end, she had to send the father weekly reports, which took 2 to 3 hours to prepare. She said, "It affected my mood in the classroom even though the principal supported me." A second-grade teacher and a fifth-grade teacher of other children in this family reported that they worried they would have to make similar reports. Other teachers also felt uncomfortable, concerned that more parents would request reports.

In Skyland the fear of blaming parents is widespread. During interviews, three teachers raised the issue of parents who blamed them for the children's problems. A teacher with less than 10 years in the district said, "We do not have the clout we did 20 [sic] years ago with the home. Fifty percent of the time I am criticized and sassed back by students that misbehave. You call the parents and they blame you for the child's behavior." Another teacher was upset because an angry parent had called the school to complain that her child had been outside in a "light mist." The mother threatened to hold the teacher responsible if the child became ill. A specialty teacher mentioned other teachers who had been blamed. She said, "The parents were complaining about what their children were not getting, not what they were."

PARENT-BLAMING

On the other hand, when teachers identify a problem with a student, they expect the parents to be involved with the solution. Teachers complained about parents failing to help them serve students. Here are a few stories supporting this claim.

A Dryden second-grade teacher related: "Some parents have a hard time with me being blunt. I had a student who could not focus, and at the time the principal and I did not see eye to eye. The student needed medication. The parents did not support that action, and several meetings were held. The parents had a second child identified as having a similar problem. The parents finally gave in and gave the medication; and the student improved. I went through hell to do it [have the student receive medication]."

An Elkin teacher provided a story about a child who was not served by the system. A teacher observed a student who had difficulty getting along with other children and remaining on task. She referred the child for EEN (exceptional educational needs) help. She was upset both with the parent's reaction to the referral and with the M-team (multidisciplinary team). The teacher believed the child was CD (Cognitively Delayed) and ED (emotionally disturbed). The M-team removed the child from the teacher's room and made an LD (learning disability) placement, which caused the child to regress. Both the classroom teacher and the EEN teacher confirmed the results of this placement. The classroom teacher blamed the parents for not accepting a CD or ED placement, and reported being fearful of interacting with the parents.

Other teachers from Elkin reported similar problems with parents who did not take responsibility for their children. A second-grade teacher reported that parents pressure teachers into not retaining children. She argued, "Not to retain causes problems for the child; therefore, the school is not focused on the child's needs as they should be."

A fifth-grade teacher, with less than 5 years in the district, believes that the newcomers to the community do not support the learning of all children. She said, "In my classes we do a lot of role-playing, dividing into teams or rotation games, and peer work. I found an interesting thing: the upper students do not want to work with the lower-end students.... In some instances that is the way they are taught by the parents."

A Skyland fourth-grade teacher was observed making a phone call to a parent. She explained her relationship with the child to the parent: "I like your son.... I am determined he will have a great year." The teacher wanted the parent's help and needed to meet with him or her. The parent refused to come in to the school, which frustrated the teacher. She said, "We need to increase his [the student's] self-esteem," hoping to encourage the parent to meet with her. The parent said that the self-esteem problem had started in first grade, and asked for specific examples of the child's behavior. The teacher did not provide examples in the phone conversation, but invited the parent to the open house. In a follow-up conversation, the teacher told the author that the parent had not come in to talk with her. The teacher said, "This boy needs all your [the parent's] help," and expressed disappointment because she did not have the parent's support.

A teacher who had overheard the previous phone conversation said, "Sometimes parents just don't understand. Parents feel it is the teacher's fault if the child is not learning.... Teachers and parents must work together for the child's benefit to find solutions.... This problem was never resolved and the child went on to the next teacher. She had similar problems." The teacher reported using the guidance counselor and psychologist to help get the parent involved.

STUDENTS

Teachers in all schools report that students bring their social environment to school. This disrupts the teachers' vision of themselves as classroom teachers providing good classrooms. Teachers are concerned about students from dysfunctional families, who are discipline problems and who create special needs in their classrooms. Each student's problem makes it more difficult for the teacher to maintain his or her vision.

Dysfunctional Families

Children from dysfunctional families need someone who cares about them. They require extra help in learning social skills. Teachers are concerned that parents will criticize them for spending inadequate amounts of time with their children. Comparing the teachers' attitudes about the needs of students from dysfunctional families suggests some teachers see themselves as an extension of the home; others do not see this as part of the responsibility of teaching.

Teachers find themselves in a role other than that of teacher. Children bring their problems to school, which affects teachers' their ability to teach. A Dryden kindergarten teacher said, "I see sad children coming in the classroom, having experience beyond their years." She reports taking time to support these children by building their self-esteem. She supported her action stating, "They are difficult to manage and need love and care. We need to give kids a good sense of self-worth. I have been more like a mom to some of these kids." Another teacher said, "Students fail because there is no family guidance."

An Elkin teacher said, "Kids are coming to school with baggage from home we don't understand. We don't really know any way to solve the problem [dysfunctional families]. There is not an easy answer." A teacher reported talking to a student who claimed he was going to run away from home. The teacher said, "I wanted another person with me to verify what was going on.... The child repeated the story and added that I could not tell anyone, because someone will come and take him away. The child said his dad said he would shoot anyone that tried to take him. 'He would even kill a cop.'" Other teachers confirmed this story. The problem was reported to Social Services, which did intervene. The teachers involved said they were concerned about what the father would do, but so far nothing has happened to the teachers or the school.

Teachers at Elkin view parents as among the reasons students do poorly in school. A teacher asked, "Who is accountable? How do you teach the parents? In some cases the parents are the problem." She claimed a student of hers "ran the parents" and wanted to also run her classroom. Another teacher blamed parents for not staying home and making sure the kids ate breakfast before they came to school. She said, "Students have their head on the desk or are lethargic and cannot stick to the lesson. After milk break, we find improvement. You see, that's society." She estimated that about 15% of her students had this problem. Other teachers confirmed that students bring family problems to school and that 10 to 15% of the class have difficulty functioning before milk break.

Teachers at Skyland claim that changes in the structure of their students' families require that they use class time to teach social skills. One teacher reported that one-fourth of her children come from single-parent homes. Another teacher said, "Kids are needy. I do not have control over divorce or families. I was not prepared in school to know how to motivate kids like these. Several students are struggling through the day because of social issues." One teacher mentioned several students from single-parent families who don't get along with others in the classroom or on the playground. She claims these students see too much of each other, because their parents send them to the same place for care before and after school.

One teacher was in the lounge every morning when her students were arriving. One day she told the author, "I hide in here until after announcements. I cannot stand having 20 kids coming in and telling me what happened last night or this morning." She explained that the kids do not get attention at home, so they want someone to listen to them.

Discipline

Students who are discipline problems threaten teachers' mental models of the well-disciplined classroom. The concern is these students will affect the teachers' reputations as good teachers and reduce the teachers' status with other teachers, administrators, parents, and the community.

When teachers talked about student discipline problems, they related them to family issues or special needs. Students who disrupt the classroom reduce the time teachers can spend helping other students. The researcher asked a Dryden teacher why she took action to control misbehaving students assigned to her class. She responded, "They disrupt your room." When asked how she deals with disruptive students, she said, "I can pass them on to [the superintendent/principal]."

Dryden teachers are concerned with discipline during the school day. They perceive discipline problems outside the classroom as social problems. A teacher said, "Students are coming to school without breakfast, without sleep, and ready to fight. Those are concerns that get in the way of so many kids." Another teacher said, "It seems like we are teaching more and more social skills, so students can work in groups of two or three, and large groups. We are spending time in class taking care of getting along, sharing, showing respect for each other and authority, manners, individual relationships and self-concepts." A teacher dealing with similar problems said, "You have a lack of support that distracts from teaching. Yet it is my responsibility to teach the child. I am not giving up. I haven't found the right tools yet."

In Skyland, disciplinary problems were a common topic of conversation in the teachers' lounge, in the halls, and at a teachers' meeting. A teacher who supported the conservative group said, "The school year has not started well. The teachers have been having discipline problems and the teachers are uneasy not knowing what is going to happen." The principal said she had been dealing with discipline problems since the first day of school. She maintained records of discipline referrals, which revealed a dramatic drop from the beginning of this school year to November.

During observations by the researcher, students behaved well. Nonetheless, both the janitor and a specialty teacher commented to the researcher on the students' poor behavior one morning. The researcher saw one student swing a bag while walking down the hall to his locker. Other students, however, walked directly to their lockers and went to their rooms. It was possible to talk in the halls without raising one's voice.

The principal of Skyland's elementary school claimed that teachers who supported the conservative group on the board were making an issue of discipline. She said, "I have the data to support discipline is not a problem, but I don't know if they will accept it." As the researcher was leaving the office, a teacher, who supports the conservative group, brought a student in and said to the principal, "This student was lying on the floor in the lunch line; you have to deal with him. Discipline is so bad." The teacher left the office, leaving the researcher to wonder why she had not sent the student to the classroom teacher, or handled the problem herself.

Two Skyland teachers talked about discipline problems in the classroom. A teacher supportive of the liberal group said, "There are times when I have to deal with discipline. I have…four that are constant discipline problems." He explained how he handled the problems and said he believed he was making progress, but that it took time away from other students. A teacher supportive of the conservative group was involved with planning a group outing, and placed all of the discipline problems in a single group. On the day of the outing she told another teacher, "All the kids that don't want to come to school are in that group."

Regardless of the circumstances surrounding student discipline, teachers are concerned. They report that principals and parents judge them on how well behaved their classrooms are. A teacher who has taught several grade levels in three schools over 28 years still fears classroom disruptions. She recalled for the researcher that as a new teacher she got all of the "bad kids." This condition almost caused her to quit teaching, because parents and teachers felt she could not handle children. The following year she worked to ensure that would not happen again. She is now thought of as a good teacher; however, in the spring she spends time negotiating who will be in her classes. The point is, it made no difference to the parents or other teachers that she had difficult students. She was still expected to have classroom discipline that matched the vision of parents and teachers. Unfair? Most people would think so, but that is the reality.

Special Needs Students

The number of special needs students has increased in each school, and teachers are concerned that inclusion programs will place even more special needs students in their classrooms. Teachers reported two reasons for their concern: they are not trained to teach special needs children and these children distract them from teaching academic subjects to other children. Both circumstances place teachers at risk of losing status because others (parents, teachers, and administration) may perceive them as failing to measure up to their visions of "good teachers." At the same time, the researcher knows 12 to 20% of students have some special need. This suggests that student population needs have changed; this is now a common cause issue. Yet school structures treat special needs as a special cause.

Dryden teachers were concerned about the increase in the number of EEN students. A first-grade teacher said, "It seems like more students every year qualify for special help." The counselor and superintendent/principal verified that the number of special needs students has increased steadily over the past 5 years.

A Dryden teacher questioned whether mainstreaming such children will meet their needs. She said, "I have concerns of budget cuts to LD and ED students."

An Elkin special education teacher is concerned about not helping students. She said, "I have worked at [the school] for 2 years. I want to change, because ED kids are the most hated kids in school. I feel I cannot be effective in helping them."

An Elkin specialty teacher said, "I have restrictions with mainstreaming children, especially wheelchairs." She reported that handicapped children interfere with other students' learning, and said she would like all handicapped children in one class. She felt this would benefit both handicapped and nonhandicapped students, and claimed she would be willing to teach an additional class each week for handicapped students if the administration would let her.

Elkin teachers did not talk about EEN students unless asked. Their comments did not reflect concern with current special education procedures, and they said they did not know how inclusion would affect them.

Two Skyland teachers talked about students with special educational needs. A split-grade-level teacher said, "There are a lot of students who need special help that takes a lot of time.... I take this personally and feel guilty that these children have such a hard time learning. I feel it is my fault. It got so bad last year that my husband told me if I cannot deal with it get out of the profession.... It's going much better this year." A third-grade teacher said, "There are more kids with special needs than ever before. You want to do your best for all kids.... I help them as much as possible in learning." He explained this took time from the others, and described a solution that he does not support: "Wouldn't it be nice to put all of those students in one class so they could not disrupt the other students, but of course this would be a problem, because those kids would not have any role models."

STATE AND NATIONAL GOVERNMENT

State and national officials will find this statement disturbing: Classroom teachers, specialty teachers, and special education teachers do not perceive that state and/or federal legislation has an impact on them. However, evidence suggests it does. In these three schools, few teachers made comments about effects of state or national government. The comments made fell into two categories: funding and mandates. Teachers were aware that state law had an impact on school funding and mandating programs, although teachers' perceptions of how varied and information from other sources did not support teachers views. Teachers were aware that Dryden's restructuring was caused by spending limits. The third-grade reading test was a state initiative. Few teachers had knowledge of how national government affected them. Teachers were not usually concerned about controls or mandates made by state or federal officials.

State Government: Funding

When Dryden teachers commented on the state government, they focused on school funding and on the governor. A first-grade teacher said, "We get state aid and I don't know anything more about that." These teachers believe that the governor controls the media, which won public support for caps on school budgets. A second-grade teacher said, "The governor, he is the one that proposed all these cuts." Teachers who mentioned the caps were concerned about two issues: wages, and supplies for their classrooms.

A negotiator for the Dryden teachers' union noted, "This [the budget caps] places a lot on their minds. A lot of teachers will be making less next year than this." When other teachers raised the wage issue, the researcher asked whether money was a reward. One replied, "It's my well-being." Another said, "No comments about salary, but I earn every penny. I reward the district and they reward me." Two other teachers thought the salary issue would become worse before it improved. The researcher discovered that contracts had not been settled for the next school year. Board members and teachers' negotiators believed that a settled contract would result in a 3% salary increase.

Dryden teachers were divided on the issue of money for supplies. Comments ranged from "Everyone has an adequate budget" to "If you don't have money you cannot make improvements." Teachers who reported adequate supplies had not changed their teaching methods. Teachers who were changing the method of instruction to "hands-on instruction" argued that their normal yearly budget was inadequate.

Elkin teachers generally did not perceive state budget caps impacted them. Only one Elkin teacher commented on budget caps. She said, "A lot has to do with funding; everyone is fighting for more." Questioned whether that was the only impact of budget caps, she said, "That's all I know of." Other teachers knew the caps were causing problems in negotiation, but reported having supplies for their classrooms.

Skyland teachers differed in their perception of how school funding affects them. A Skyland teacher was asked, "Does the state affect your classroom?" The teacher said, "That's hard. I don't know if they are worse or better. Our current governor wants to make us a state of mediocrity in regards to education and he disregards the teachers. [The governor] is using the fact his wife and in-laws are teachers to build his credibility as a knowledgeable critic of education. He does not know about education. He is concerned about cost.... The governor's comments are hurting teachers and that reflects on the students. The reflections are caused by teachers not feeling good about themselves.... It is a loss of personal worth.... I would like to see the state provide more resources to schools and be more supportive." Other Skyland teachers reported similar feelings. A first-grade teacher said, "The caps on teachers' salaries have affected teachers' attitudes, caps on building spending; you have to make choices between programs that are good for all kids." A special education teacher said, "We are more criticized now than we have ever been. The governor has used his family to build a belief he is knowledgeable. I don't feel he is." She discussed the state aid formula and how the caps affected the district, but she gave no answer when she was asked about specific effects on the district.

The district reduced the superintendent's proposed 1994–1995 budget by $700,000, resulting in a real increase of 5% (after inflation) over the previous year. The superintendent reported that the budget for teachers' supplies remained virtually the same, at the building level, as in previous years. He cut costs by reducing aides' (educational assistants') time, resulting in a 50% reduction in CTC time (CTC is an acronym teachers use to describe a planning meeting held once a month during the school day; however, when asked to expand the acronym, several teachers and a principal could not do so), cutting extended day kindergarten and the strings program. Teachers said, "Supplies were cut," although the principal confirmed the superintendent's comment that budgets for supplies remained unchanged from the previous year.

State Government: Mandates

When Dryden classroom teachers were asked, "Does the state affect you?" the standard answer was "yes." When asked how, teachers would cite mandated testing or minutes of instruction. But teachers did not know the required minutes of instruction for a particular subject area such as reading, math, or science. Regarding mandated testing, a second-grade teacher said, "The third-grade reading test, everyone was really worried. When the test came, they thought it was pretty average." She explained, "Teachers had anxiety at first, but dropped it after they saw the test." The third-grade teacher interviewed did not mention the test until asked. Her students score well, so she was not concerned.

Dryden special education teachers discussed a special education mandate called "inclusion." One classroom teacher suggested that inclusion was being mandated "to save money and meet the state requests." Both special education and classroom teachers talked about inclusion of special education students into the regular education classrooms. They expressed concern that they would not receive training on how to carry out the program or on the program's expectations. A special education teacher said, "The classroom teacher needs material to teach the special needs children. Without the supplies and resources, teachers will look like they are opposed to inclusion." Other teachers were unable to describe what the inclusion mandate meant; some did not know that the district is moving toward inclusion. One regular education teacher is concerned about the implementation of "504 plans" that address the needs of students who do not qualify for EEN programs but have identifiable barriers to learning. He said, "You just are not sure what you are to be doing, but no one really knows what to do."

Elkin teachers raised the issue of state mandates and reported that they affect their classrooms. A second-grade teacher said, "There are these mandates and these are all stressors. It is difficult to be focused solely on student learning." Other teachers reported similar feelings. A first-grade teacher said, "We have the state mandates, third-grade reading test, and minutes of instruction for subject areas." One classroom teacher plus the special education teachers supported the state mandate requiring inclusion of special education students in regular classrooms. A teacher who did not support inclusion said, "Mainstreaming learning problems in the classroom, you need more adult supervision. With 25 to 30 kids in the classroom you don't have time to work with these kids." She had one severely handicapped child in her room.

Most Elkin teachers could not say how state mandates affected them. One teacher said, "I don't follow them." Teachers reported concern about the third-grade reading test, when as a group the students' scores fell below 90%. The teacher who said she had "25 to 30" students in her room was asked how many students she usually has. She said, "The most was 25, the least was 18." Teachers commonly said that the state interfered with instruction.

Skyland teachers reported that state mandates affect the school, but could not explain how the mandates improved the school or student learning. A special education teacher said, "Absolutely, we use the DPI [Department of Public Instruction] as a resource.... People were contacted for information and two workshops. They set up the third-grade reading test, and now the fourth- and eighth-grade tests. They [the state government] are innovative in getting new programs into the school." A classroom teacher said, "Probably, I am not sure they [mandates] have improved schools, special education maybe. [The school district] has always been good with the standards. I just don't know how much.... The administration would know more about that." Another classroom teacher said, "The third-grade reading test is one. Now they [the state] are doing fourth, eighth, and tenth. I am sure eventually it [the state] will [improve schools]. It did not affect third-grade." When the researcher probed for specifics on how the state standards affect teachers, teachers could did not comment.

NATIONAL GOVERNMENT AND MEDIA

Two Dryden teachers expressed concern about the national media's treatment of education. A special education teacher said, "It is a community status issue. The teachers are now being scapegoated. The higher the power and status, the greater the scapegoating. When teachers struggle against the social forces, then they want to find a safe place." A teacher with 30 years in the classroom said, "The president's comments put down teachers, when teachers are doing the best job they can do with what they have." Other Dryden teachers were questioned about the national media and government. These teachers either expressed no concern, or explicitly suggested that national issues did not concern them.

The researcher asked Elkin teachers, "Does the national government or national issues affect you as a classroom teacher?" Two teachers responded, "No, I don't think so" and "They do not affect me." One teacher argued, "We have the federal mandates that have to be addressed: sexuality, gender, race, and religion.

All taking another set of teachers' time away from the classroom.... These are all in separate committees that are set up." Other Elkin teachers did not comment on national issues.

Skyland teachers generally did not raise concerns about national issues. One teacher said, "On TV we are getting blasted all of the time. Families need to feel comfortable about the school." The researcher probed for possible effects of the federal government and national issues, but teachers gave no response.

CLOSING COMMENTS ON THE EXTERNAL ENVIRONMENT

This chapter concludes the discussion of how the cultures of the external environment dimension affect teachers' attitudes toward school improvement. Systems thinking suggests that at least five major factors in the external environment affect school improvement: community/community members, parents, students, state government, and national government. Within each of these categories there are endless possibilities of subcategories, which can contribute to patterns of behaviors and processes. In studying your own school, these factors will provide the framework within which you can discover the key patterns that affect your school. But Chapters 5 and 6 covered only one dimension! There are five others to explore.

CHAPTER 7

The Closed Culture

INTRODUCTION

This chapter suggests that schools are being strangled by a closed educational system. The internal environment culture dimension is created by forces generated here and in the other five dimensions (the culture of the external environment, formal and informal leadership, strategies, structure, and results). Activities carried out and/or blocked in each dimension have taught teachers to protect what they value, their vision of a good classroom.

This concept of a closed educational system goes beyond the traditional ideas about organizational climate. Such ideas refer to the atmosphere within the school (the school's culture) and to the behaviors that influence people (including how individuals relate to one another). In contrast, systems thinking recognizes that everything that occurs in each part of the system affects the organization's internal culture. The case studies from Dryden, Elkin, and Skyland demonstrate why school employees are cautious about carrying out changes, even innovative ideas designed to improve student learning. In each community, anything that threatens social ranking places individuals at risk of being labeled a "poor teacher." Even using rewards to build status for maintaining or enhancing their own or another's power is risky. To avoid this label, teachers work hard and seek to maintain their place in a strong informal social ranking system that protects their vision of a good classroom.

The internal culture includes all people within an organization. There is a fine line between the culture of the external environment and that of the internal environment. For example, board candidates belong to the external culture until they take office and join the internal environment. Volunteers are external until specific individuals become a common part of the school's regular processes. A one-time volunteer may help on a given day, but her assistance has minimal impact on school operations; therefore, she is considered external. All regular employees and volunteers of the school district, paid and unpaid, are part of the internal culture.

The question of whether students belong to the internal or external culture may be debated. Of course, students do affect the operations of the school district, individual schools, and classrooms; however, students are the people schools are designed to serve. The impact students have on teachers, as discussed in Chapters 5 and 6, suggests that students belong to the external culture. Teachers describe their students as products of the external environment. They cite examples of dysfunctional families, and the student's role as part of such a family. In some cases teachers report that students disrupt their vision of themselves as classroom teachers.

When we use systems theory to consider the culture of the internal environment, we take a systemic view of all human interaction within the schools, examining how school employees and other members of the internal culture relate among themselves and with the other five dimensions of the organizational system. This chapter will compare Dryden, Elkin, and Skyland, using general categories related to the internal culture: social structure, support system, competition, being valued in decision-making, individual acceptance, trust in administrative leadership, hardworking staff, and poor teacher.

INTERNAL ENVIRONMENT CULTURE

Social Structure

The social structure shows and describes teachers in relationship with other teachers, all school employees, and external factors, parents and community groups. The social structure is a "closed social system" in which informal leadership uses power, status, sanctions, and rewards to control and mandate individual or group compliance, to support their vision of a good school. Each school's structure is different, but each seems to match the community's political power structure. Understanding how a closed system develops and why it is maintained requires systems thinking.

The social order drives the organizational culture. The system is driven by power and influence; as a result, individuals and groups use power (force, domination, and/or manipulation) to dictate the performance of particular acts or commands that alter the behavior of others (Goldhamer and Shils, 1939). These findings support Bowles's (1993a,b) claim that within a political system individuals and groups protect what they value. He offers two models, "Analysis of Political Policy" and "Power and Influence" (Mauriel, 1989), to explain how the political system works to protect what an individual or group values. The culture expects teachers to conform to its values and norms.

Such findings suggest that when teachers do not conform to the culture, they place at risk their persons, professional lives, and visions. Therefore, they must focus on power, status, reward, and well-being to survive in the system.

Teachers who do not conform are forced out of the school or pushed outside the social structure.

For example, changes in teaching staffs in Dryden disrupted the social structure, and teachers reported being treated as outsiders. In Elkin, the administration reported that new teachers were ostracized and a teacher was forced out of the school because other teachers would not accept her. In Skyland, the principal complained of being forced to have teachers on the hiring team. To some observers, these teachers appear cold and rigid, but this stance protects the teachers' visions. Unless they create a strong social structure, teachers are left to stand alone.

The internal social structure provides a means for teachers to protect their visions. Teachers who have power to control the decision-making process use others to maintain or enhance their visions. Teachers who align themselves closely with the powerful leaders receive personal, professional, and vision protection.

Dryden

Dryden's restructuring forced teachers to move to different schools. These teachers reported feeling rejection from established teachers. They reported being excluded from social activities such as parties for holidays and retirements. One teacher said, "I felt we were treated as outsiders." This was verified by other people new to the building.

The administration reported it was pressured into including teachers on hiring teams. When the most recent teacher was hired, other teachers from that grade level were part of the hiring team. The superintendent/principal explained, "They know the administration is going to be gone. I will not be here. This pressures them to band together to survive."

Dryden's sociogram (Fig. 7.1) maps the lines of influence between school employees. The diagram shows the lines of influence between individuals and employee groups. A few staff members (solitary x's) do not interact with others enough to influence others within the school. The superintendent/principal has no influence other than what others permit. (Note the support staff's strong influence over the superintendent/principal.)

One individual, Lori D1, directly or indirectly influences everyone in the school. A second teacher, Lisa D2, has similarly extensive influence, but is influenced by Lori D1. Teachers Lori D1 and Lisa D2 believe they are always focused on improving student learning; they claim they never seek power, status, or rewards, or concern themselves about their own well-being. However, their observed actions suggest they maintain power and status, and control the decision-making process in the school, so that it coincides with their beliefs about school structure and vision.

For example, Lori D1 was one of three people in the district not moved in the restructuring. The researcher asked her, "What would have happened if you

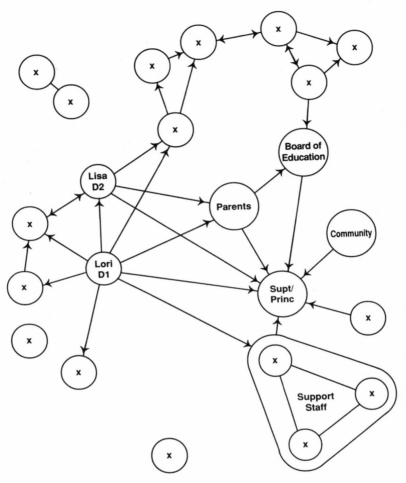

Figure 7.1. Dryden's sociogram.

were moved?" She said, "I would have gone after [the superintendent/principal]." She stopped talking until the researcher repeated her statement, and added she "would have found a way to deal with that. It [not being moved] has made other relationships difficult. I have been told to my face, 'the squeaky wheel gets the grease.'" Lisa D2 supported the staff moves because she was moved to a better room. One or both of these teachers are always selected to serve on decision-making committees. Both are very active with parents and talk to the superintendent/principal two to four times each day, building support for anything they want to occur.

Elkin

Teachers who are established in the Elkin school do not interact with new certified teachers or parents not active in the PTO. The established teachers did not openly avoid new staff members, but did not share with them, ask them to join conversations in the lounge, or sit at the same table. As a result, new teachers did not spend time in the lounge, and sat alone when eating. When an established teacher went on an educational trip, she returned with food and a photo album. All teachers and support staff shared the food, reviewed the book, and asked questions. A week later a new teacher attended a workshop. She placed a book she had purchased and other materials in the lounge, with an explanatory note. Not one person looked at the materials. Three days later, the materials were on a shelf.

An administrator told a story, confirmed by a teacher, of how a new teacher had been forced out of the school in one year. The principal hired the teacher from another state. He believed she was an outstanding, creative, and innovative teacher, based on her references. The principal reported that the staff did not accept her: "The staff was upset they were not involved in the hiring and they did everything to make it hard for her." In response to the pressure, the teacher left at the end of the year. The principal said, "I do not like having teachers on the hiring team," but claims if he does not, the teachers will not let new people in. He says the system will not change because the teachers hire people like themselves; he cannot change the system by bringing in new people.

Elkin's sociogram (Fig. 7.2) maps the lines of influence between school employees. The diagram shows groups of teachers connected by association within and outside of school. Teacher Kathy E1 has the greatest influence on a group based on religious association outside of school. Teachers Ruth E2 and Marge E3 have the greatest influence with groups based on long-time associations with the school. The group that includes Mary E4 is linked by their location in the building and social relationships outside of school. Four staff members (solitary x's) have no influence with other staff members.

Kathy E1 influences everyone in the school system, directly or indirectly. Ruth E2 has similarly extensive influence, except on Kathy E1. Teachers Marge E3, Mary E4, and Ann E5 influence others who support their autonomy in their classrooms. The principal has no influence other than that promoted by others. It is interesting to note that the PTO has great influence over the principal; other lines of influence originate from Kathy E1, Ruth E2, Marge E3, and Mary E4.

Kathy E1 and Ruth E2 believe they are always focused on improving student learning, but their actions suggest they work at maintaining power to control the decision-making process. Marge E3 and Mary E4 state, "I am always focused on improving student learning, but others [teachers] are concerned about power, personal status, reward, and well-being." A specialty teacher, Ann E5, reported a similar feeling and said, "I see it [concern about power...] for others,

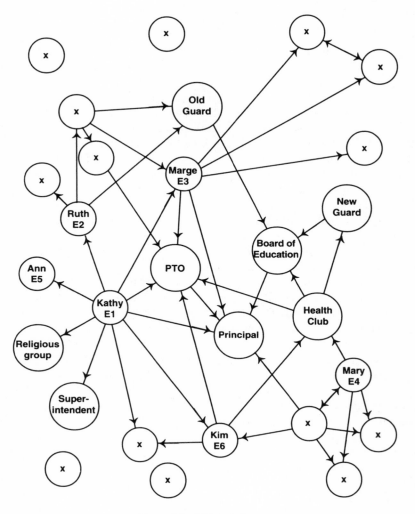

Figure 7.2. Elkin's sociogram.

not for me, but committees, parents, and family take me away from focusing on the students."

The principal's comment about Kathy E1 confirms the line of influence in the diagram. He said, "[Kathy E1] uses the PTO in an underhanded way. She controls the PTO. She is allied on the surface, but she is not. She is excellent at controlling parents.... [Kathy E1] can keep it the way she wants. It gets to me sometimes." Kathy E1 uses Kim E6 to control the PTO and the membership. In the lounge, Kim E6 talked about holding a meeting during suppertime and requiring that each person bring a personal salad to eat. Reviewing the attendance list of the meeting suggests the meeting time and menu caused exclusion of non-PTO parents. This meeting established the Awards Day program. A new teacher later said, "The awards went to all the PTO kids."

The PTO and health club memberships overlapped. The new liberal board member, PTO president, Mary E4, and Kim E6 are all active long-time members of the health club. The board member and the president of the PTO are best friends.

Marge E3 talks to individual PTO members, but is not active in the meetings. She has developed a high degree of personal status by winning local, state, and national awards for innovations. In the lounge, she talked about changes in her classroom without being challenged by others. Both board members interviewed commented that she was a strong teacher.

Skyland

Teachers who are established in the school interact with other established teachers, but are fearful of strangers and so do not interact with new certified teachers. Yet an established teacher said, "We have a great climate in our school. People are happy, professional. They share. It is a very healthy school." Another established teacher said, "We're not real cliquey here. We do wonderful things with the Sunshine Fund. We share ideas. We like to see other people share their ideas."

This upbeat perception is not necessarily shared by the administration or supported by data. An administrator said, "I feel the school has become a very vicious place. Two teachers...are aligned with the [conservative] group.... [The new board member] claims several teachers have called her asking her to make [the administrators] stop what they are doing." In another meeting, the administrator reported that other staff members work well together. Observation of this meeting suggested that the few powerful teachers work together and exclude others.

Observation suggests that the established staff does not easily accept new teachers or new ideas. A particular teacher with less than 5 years' experience (one of the lone xs in Fig. 7.3) belongs to no group. Teachers don't converse with her in the lounge or hallways. Unless she is in a planning meeting, she remains by herself. Another new teacher stays in her room during lunch and prep times. No established teacher was ever observed in the room either newcomer. An established teacher said, "I remember when you crossed an old-timer there was 'hell' to pay."

Teachers have pressured past administrators into placing them on hiring teams. The current principal approves of this practice, explaining, "The new teachers have a support system."

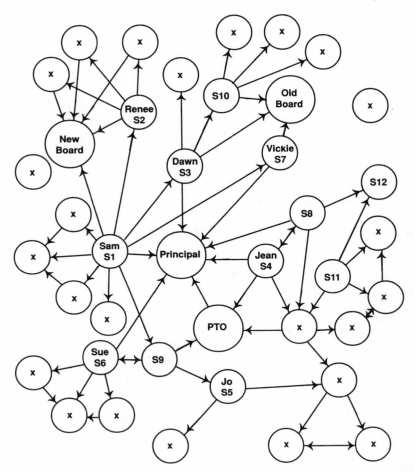

Figure 7.3. Skyland's sociogram.

Established teachers are fearful of strangers in the building. The staff were wary of the researcher, for example. One teacher said, "It's a lack of trust with strangers. You're going to be here for a short time and leave and so no one knows what is going to happen." Later in the day, the principal told the researcher, "I have had questions about who you are and 'what is he doing when he is taking notes?'" Two weeks after the researcher was in the building, the principal requested an explanatory memo to place in the school's bulletin, and asked the researcher to wear a visitor's badge. An established teacher, Renee S2 commented, "It is not you, it is the effects of last spring's election. No one knows what is going to happen."

Skyland's sociogram (Fig. 7.3) maps the lines of influence between school employees and the community. The diagram shows groups of teachers, connected by associations within the school. Groups influenced by teachers Sam S1, Renee S2, Dawn S3, Jean S4, Jo S5, and Sue S6 are naturally occurring groups that teach common grade levels (kindergarten to fifth grade), specialty programs, or special education. Notice two solitary xs for two teachers who do not belong to a group and have no influence within the school.

Sam S1 influences everyone in the school system, directly or indirectly. Renee S2 and Dawn S3 have similarly broad influence, except that they do not directly influence each other. The group influenced by Renee S2 supports the new conservative movement in the district. All other groups favor teacher autonomy, supported by liberals, as the best means of improving the district. The principal's influence derives exclusively from others.

All lines of influence originate with Sam S1, Renee S2, or Dawn S3. Sam S1 believes that all teachers focus on improving student learning. Renee S2 and Dawn S3 view themselves as always having a focus on student learning, but believe other teachers do not. However, the behaviors of all three teachers suggest they also work at maintaining power to control the decision-making process.

When Sam S1 was asked whether teachers focus on student learning, she said, "I never had to struggle with that.... I get to organize my class and have freedom. It is gratifying. The school operates the way I like it to operate." The researcher read to Dawn S3 the statement contrasting teacher focus on student learning with attention to their own conditions of employment. She said, "I don't think it pertains to me. It may for others. I don't like to be gone from my class. I want to spend time with the students." Renee S2 made similar comments after hearing the statement.

The principal confirmed that Renee S2 was aligned with the conservative group in the community and Dawn S3 had influence in the community. However, the principal did not know that Sam S1 had met with both the conservative group and the outgoing board members. The principal felt that any one of these three teachers was able to start or stop a change within the school.

Support System

Teachers differed from school to school in reporting need for support. This suggests that teachers who work in a stable social system do not talk about the personal and professional support it provides, but know that personal and professional support is important to survive in the system.

Personal support varied with location. In Dryden, teachers whose classrooms had been moved from a different school differed in their feelings of loss, depending on how long they had had established relationships in the previous school. Teachers reported feelings of loss for friends, and some were emotionally moved as they described the loss of teacher, parent, and community friends. In Elkin, which has a stable social structure, teachers did not talk about personal support unless asked. In response to questions, they said they valued personal support as a defense against attacks by parents and other members of the community. In Skyland, teachers who were not aligned with the conservative group reported aligning themselves with individuals and groups for personal support to cope with the new conservative group's attacks.

Teachers in all three schools reported needing professional support to be good teachers. They valued their colleagues as sources of information, support for their ideas, and help in solving problems.

The teachers' union, when active, appeared as a tool to control power, not to give support. Teachers in Dryden and Skyland viewed the union as unimportant. Dryden teachers were unaware of union activities. In Skyland, union activities focused on protecting teacher autonomy. Teachers controlled the decision-making process outside contract negotiations by dealing directly with the administration and board of education. In Elkin, a few members of the union controlled the decision-making process for determining instructional methods and contractual language. Teachers in this school were active in the union's activities, even when they did not support the union's actions.

Dryden

Teachers who talked about the need for personal support had lost contact with other teachers or support staff as a result of the changes in school grade-level structure. A teacher who had been involuntarily moved to the school at the beginning of the school year said, "[The former school] was like a family that included the parents of the students. It was like losing someone in your family. The ones who were there the longest had the hardest time." As she concluded her story she said, "Once you leave you can never go back.... You are afraid of the unknown [new school environment]. It affects your well-being." Other staff members felt the same. "It was the pits, people who moved had the hardest time."

Teachers who did not comment on the move were asked if it had affected them. If the move had benefited them or had not changed close relationships, they supported the staff changes. A special education teacher who received a larger room in a school closer to home said, "I don't have a problem leaving the school," but explained that other teachers felt bad about losing friends or their rooms.

A few teachers talked about personal support from other teachers and support staff during difficult times in their personal lives. One teacher received support from others who walked with her after school while she was recovering from a heart problem. Reactions to divorce varied from "I appreciate the time [that person] spent with me," to "I don't go to the lounge because it is too stressful."

Teachers have several sources of professional support. The most common is from other teachers. A kindergarten teacher acknowledged support from outside resources (other teachers), stating, "You just have [to have] someone to solve problems with." One teacher described problems she had keeping focused as to what her job was. She attended an in-service course for help. Although the course was centered on serving students and not on the teacher's well-being, she said, "The speaker's comments gave me permission to have fun on the job." She claimed she had not been trained to have fun and concluded, "I give myself permission to have fun so I am free to serve children."

Dryden teachers are minimally engaged in union activity. The union president said, "The union/association is very inactive. I don't know what it will take to get people involved." A teacher negotiator said, "I got into it because there were no elementary teachers in negotiations." Observation and teachers' comments verified: "I guess we don't have a problem."

Elkin

Teachers did not volunteer information about needing personal support from other staff members until they were specifically asked about it. One teacher said, "The teachers would miss people, but it would not affect me. Others it would." Other teachers said, "Teachers support each other; they are concerned about you as a person and your personal life," and "We have a staff that cares." Teachers frequently said, "I haven't thought about it." Only one member of the staff had been in the school fewer than 5 years; three others have less than 10 years in the school. This staff stability suggests that teachers have little experience with loss of personal support.

Teachers responded to questions of professional support when asked. Teachers who had received support were positive about other teachers. A teacher who reported having her ideas rejected felt unsupported. One teacher reported receiving support in handling a parent complaint. She called this "a two-way street" because the other teachers were directly affected by the situation, and said "They were definitely a support."

A special education teacher claimed she does not feel supported by classroom teachers. She wants to work with her students in the classroom because she thinks the children would make greater gains, but the regular classroom teacher have rejected her offer. She claims other teachers want the students to come to her room. She said, "It makes them look good."

Teachers are active in the union, but they differ in their view of union activities. Ruth E2 with more than 20 years in the district, said, "If it is a real issue all the teachers attend the union meetings." A teacher with less than 5 years in the district said, "The union is active. They are interested in issues that affect teachers' benefits, how things are handled by the administration, like the hiring of teachers." Another teacher gave a personal reason for her association with the union association: "I want job security."

Some teachers did not support union activities. A teacher with more than 5 years in the district argued that the union was not supportive about kids during the work slowdown over wages. She said, "According to the union...work was not to be done outside the school day." She reported feeling pressured: "I did not attend the 50-year celebration. It was an awful time for me. I would sneak in the building and work in the evenings and on Sundays." Marge E3 with 20 years in the district, reported the feelings of other teachers: Some teachers [fifth and sixth grade] are still angry about the strike.... This group thought everyone was taking advantage of them."

Interviews with administrators and board members confirmed that the union was active and that a few teachers did not support all of the union's activities. A board member said, "The biggest complaint I have with the union is they protect the poor teachers," but he would not provide examples.

Skyland

Teachers talked about the importance of having a personal support system. A specialty teacher said, "Your students, how can we best take care of their interests and needs?... The key is finding out how teachers are doing personally. Teachers need a support system." A classroom teacher said, "I feel to improve student learning, teachers need...to be taken care of. If teachers don't feel good about themselves, they won't focus on students." A teacher who was pressured by conservative parents said, "When you get scared, you're not going to be supportive of kids or improving student learning."

Teachers talked about supporting other teachers. One teacher said, "I feel sorry for other teachers...I would tell them...use me as a sounding board. Last week I spent a half-hour on the phone with [another teacher]." A second teacher reported supporting a colleague who was having problems with parents. When the researcher asked this teacher about the pressure, she became emotional and started to cry.

Teachers also welcome other teachers' help in solving students' problems. A split-grade-level teacher said, "Our 4/5 team is supportive of each other. There is usually someone on the team who is usually supportive of an idea. So you are not working alone. This year I do not have any special education students, but usually the special education teacher gets involved and helps us...." Two teachers were having similar discipline problems in their classrooms. One of the teachers came into the lounge after carrying out a particular activity and told the other teacher, "I am very happy about the activity. It resolved the problem." Later, both teachers planned how to share the information with others.

Teachers reported that the union was not active, but observation suggests that the union acts to control the decision-making process. The union places information in the lounge, on the bulletin board, and on a table, about its positions on regional and state activities and issues. When a teacher was asked about the union, she said, "In this building it is unique; we have people concerned, but [we] don't have time to explore options. Only a few key people are involved. People don't come to the union meetings. We have to deal directly with the administration." A board member and the union negotiator confirmed that teachers are not active in the union. The board member said, "The teachers' union did not take a formal stand in the last election." The negotiator said, "Teachers do not attend union meetings; however, teachers are very active in developing a governance policy."

The governance policy establishes the decision-making procedure for the school district. The conservative faction has drafted a new policy placing all power with the board plus a special appointed committee of parents and community members. Teachers are concerned that this policy will reduce their ability to make professional decisions. They have drafted a plan that places the decision-making power for educational improvement with school-based committees. Copies of both policy drafts were provided in the lounge, and teachers talked about the differences during breaks and lunchtime.

Competition

Competition among teachers and between schools serves to strengthen the power structure of the school. Only five teachers in the three schools reported competition among teachers; others reported cooperation and support. However, observations indicate that the reward system feeds competition. Such rewards enhance a teacher's status among other teachers, administrators, parents, and the community. Status provides credibility for the teacher's actions, and rewards signal acceptance of these actions; therefore, teachers promote and utilize the reward system directly or indirectly to advance their agendas and protect their visions.

Dryden

Teachers report differing opinions about competition. One teacher with more than 25 years in the school said, "There is not any. We are not here to compete. Competition is for status, nothing else." Although this type of comment was common, other teachers claimed that some teachers are very competitive. The researcher identified two competitive teachers, both of whom claimed they were not competitive. Four teachers also cited them as being very competitive.

A teacher with more than 20 years in the district said, "Teachers tend to be competitive. If you're not, you cannot do more for the kids.... Status may be a

factor. Self-preservation is doing a good job and no one is going to question you."
Other teachers' comments corroborate this statement. "Teachers want to be able
to voice the way they function and it will not be taken away," according to a
special education teacher. She added, "To be heard is a reward."

Teachers like praise and view it as a reward; however, praise that affects
the status of other teachers can be harmful. According to a first-grade teacher,
teachers need praise. She said, "Teachers need to know they are special. You
need those rewards. You need that support.... Teachers need to be built up to do
their best." However, one teacher told a contrary story about praise that had
harmed her. A principal placed her in front of the staff as an example of a good
teacher, saying that others should follow her example. This was very threatening
to the other teachers. She said, "I don't think anyone spoke to me for about 3
months. I did not feel like coming to school any more. I felt like I was on the
outside."

Teachers relate status to how often parents request them as their children's
teachers. Four kindergarten teachers, observed in their activities before the
kindergarten screening (identifies students' learning needs and ability to function
with others), differed significantly. The two who were identified as highly
competitive decorated their rooms by personally cutting, assembling, and hang-
ing room decorations. Each of their rooms was organized and coordinated. The
two teachers who were not competitive had the students cut or tear, assemble,
and help hang the room decorations. The rooms were organized, but the decorations were not near perfect. The two competitive teachers received parent
requests for placement of children. One of the noncompetitive teachers did not
receive any parent requests. As a result, this individual feels insecure. The other
noncompetitive teachers said, "It was not fair, she was new to the school and
parents did not know her. She is a good teacher."

Officially, the school does not honor parent requests. A board member said,
"I was not aware that teachers were aware that we accepted parent requests."
The superintendent/principal set up a system that required a letter from the
parents to make a request. The other administrator said, "I don't support the
practice of parent requests. It is a public evaluation based on personality. It is
more important who you know." Later the researcher observed the practice of
favoritism. Because of an overload in the competitive teacher's class, a difficult
student whose parent had requested the competitive teacher was moved to a
noncompetitive teacher's class list.

Teachers report that the competition decreases at higher grade levels, but
teachers claim parent requests track students through a specific set of teachers.
The tracking appears to be correlated with the relationships to parents of students
of the competitive teachers.

Teachers report different types of competition between schools within the
district. A second- and third-grade teacher feels the elementary school budget
gets cut when money is short, and the high school and middle school remain

unaffected. Another teacher said, "[Our school has] a reputation for being troublemakers." She seemed proud of this, and commented, "I know new people have a problem with that." A teacher upset with another elementary school in the district said, "They were used to being in their own little kingdom." All teachers believed their school was better than other schools in their own and neighboring districts.

Elkin

When teachers were asked about competition within the school they generally reported their colleagues as sharing or cooperative. However, awards cause teachers to feel uncomfortable. The researcher asked a teacher directly, "Is there competition between teachers?" She answered, "I don't think of it as competition. The staff is supportive of each other and share a collegial relationship to support student learning." Another teacher answered the same question by saying, "To a minor extent. I have observed more in other buildings. Our building is more cooperative and helpful." The principal reported that teachers share information. Observations and interviews suggested that teachers did not compete openly for status.

Teachers generally did not talk openly about awards, but individuals differ about their value. One individual, Marge E3, has received several awards, and most of the staff celebrate her success. Two staff members felt she was lucky, but were reluctant to say why. The researcher observed that when the award-winning teacher brought materials to the lounge, other staff members looked at and talked about the information. When the two staff members who had called her "lucky" brought materials, no one looked at them and they slowly made their way to a shelf where they remained.

Some teachers supported and others rejected action taken to recognize retirees. The PTO had started a plaque to recognize teachers, but it was not up to date. In 1994, a retiring teacher wanted the plaque up-dated. Although this was done, a support staff member reported that many teachers had not wanted the person's name there and tried to have the plaque removed rather than up-dated.

One teacher commented on an award she had received: "I don't think competition is against other teachers.... I have been nominated twice for the award.... I would have turned it down if a parent had not nominated me.... I felt uncomfortable turning down these parents, because I thought the parent would say to others I was ungrateful."

Between schools, the teachers claim that competition starts with the principals. A teacher said, "I don't know what it is everyone scrambles for the most. [The principal] gets bent out of shape on competition. Competition starts with the principals. Who has more pictures in the paper. [The principal] feeds on the competition with the principal at [two other buildings]." Another teacher reported that competition is not limited to schools within the district. She said, "The principals are competitive between the schools in the area. They brought it on themselves, with pressure from the parents or community members." The principal confirmed that principals compete for numbers of winning science fair projects and that they track test results in the area.

Skyland

When teachers were asked, "Is there competition between staff members?" a representative response was, "I don't feel there is." However, not all teachers felt this way. One teacher said, "Yes, I find that to be one of the hardest things about working here. One of the hardest things was moving from progress reports to portfolios. There was no set of guidelines to follow. So teachers started feeling they had to do more and more. It became competitive. No one wants to be the teacher that gave the parents less than another teacher." A split-grade-level teacher said, "Teachers did not want to be held accountable for something other teachers were doing and they were not." A specialty teacher who promotes the use of portfolios said, "I didn't hear about it as competition. We are aware of the problems and that is why we developed a framework that best represents the child. We are taking it slow to bring the parents and community in along with us." But a classroom teacher felt the school had moved too fast. She said, "This caused us to lose the support of the parents."

Teachers did not talk about other forms of competition; however, teachers' behavior before school opened in the fall suggested competition. One teacher was labeling each locker with a cut-out bee showing the student's name. She had decorated her room in a fall theme with paper leaves and trees. The teacher in the next room said, "I haven't done anything with the lockers." Two days later, this teacher was gluing eyes on alligator cut-outs attached to the students' lockers. From kindergarten to second grade, the rooms were filled with hand-made decorations and well organized. Teachers in third- to fifth-grade class-rooms decorated their rooms with purchased materials that had educational themes.

The researcher did not find a formal reward system for teachers in Skyland; however, observation suggests an informal reward system exists. Four teachers used the informal reward system to protect their educational programs. A teacher with 20 years in the district had been trained to teach a special reading program. Other teachers at the same grade level depend on her to help struggling students from their classes. In fact, her colleagues and the principal would like to hire a part-time teacher to give her more time to teach reading. The teacher said, "I am trying to work this into a part-time retirement position." This idea excited the principal, who said, "That would be wonderful if she does." Another teacher protected her math program using similar strategies.

The teacher who brought the split-grade-level concept into the district is viewed as an authority by her colleagues and the principal. The teacher used her status to gain special favors from other staff members. For example, she selected her own student group and topic for a grade level project. Other teachers did not question her independence, but did negotiate their own assigned duties with other teachers.

A specialty teacher is held in high esteem because she has developed a schedule that ensures that all teachers send their students to all specialty classes an equal number of times during the year. In return, classroom teachers supported her proposal for a parents' night project that required their help.

Teachers and administrators promote their school district as the best in the area. A teacher said, "[Our school] has a reputation of being on the cutting edge. The administration and teachers push hard to maintain that.... I would like to say OK, let's lighten up about it. It is better to set high expectations than low ones, but you need the support of the people, or you will burn out." Another teacher said, "The district has a reputation it tries to live up to, that is, [ours] is a district where teachers are overachievers. This places such high expectations on them that they self-impose a standard. [Our school] has a reputation of being on the cutting edge." The principal said, "One of the characteristics of teachers is they are perfectionists and support the idea that [this] is a great school district." When teachers were questioned about the differences between schools in the district, they talked about the community's impact on their school.

Being Valued in Decision-Making

Being valued in the decision-making process is a form of reward. A teacher, Lori D1, close to the administration in Dryden said it best: "It [recognition] makes you feel good. Everyone likes a warm fuzzy now and then. It's a validation. It makes you different from the other people." Later in the interview she said, "The praise one gets from other people or administration is limited." In contrast, a teacher in Skyland said, "The big thing is if people don't respect your professional judgment. If they do not respect you, where is your professional judgment? I wish people trusted us more." These contrasting statements indicate that teachers feel rewarded when they are part of the decision-making process. This can be used to sanction others. The data suggest that any form of recognition from administrators, teachers, and others builds teachers' professional status.

Dryden

A specialty teacher told a story about her introduction to the staff. At a staff meeting, the principal said, "We are so lucky to have a [title of speciality]." She said the introduction made her feel good. Another teacher complained, "There is no reward system. Rewards are compliments and feedback from other teachers, parents, and administration." The researcher probed, "Is this a rewards system?" She replied, "It probably is. When a teacher feels their opinion is valued, this causes you to share." A teacher with 20 years' experience in teaching and 15 years' experience in the district, who is not close to the administration, said, "I would like to see a lot more done to show teachers respect. That they were the experts and experienced. I have felt this way for a long time and nobody listens."

Teachers believe the administration does not value them when considering school improvements. A teacher said, "They bypass the best stuff they have, the teachers." One teacher became emotional talking about the recent changes. With tears in her eyes she said, "All the years of teaching, why didn't they set down and ask me? I am not being respected for training and experience. I was left out of helping."

Teachers feel good when they accomplish tasks with others, and feel rejected when their ideas are not considered. Two teachers reported working on a team to develop a grade-level curriculum. They agreed, "It was very satisfying to work in a group like that." In another group, a teacher had a different experience. She said, "There is peer pressure to do things the same and to resist new ideas. The people did not want to give me a chance. I learned to keep my mouth shut even if it would be better for kids. It was hard."

Elkin

Teachers did not talk about needing recognition, but their actions suggested that they seek reinforcement of their ideas from others. Teachers commonly discussed plans with the principal or with other teachers before implementing them. One teacher was observed seeking comments from the principal, other teachers, and the PTO. She asked the principal about changing her class schedule. After she left the room he turned to the researcher and said, "I don't know why she asked me that. She is going to do it anyway." Her subsequent actions seeking comments in the lounge and contacts with the PTO suggested this was her way to build support before carrying out her plans. Other teachers made similar contacts with teachers and/or the principal. One said, "In my own classroom, I would just do it. If I had a question I would talk to other teachers, then the principal."

Teachers like to be recognized for their contributions. A teacher said, "What surprised me was when I was asked to work with the playground aides to help with playground problems, I was encouraged [by the teachers and principal] to do it [reduce student conflict]. This meant my kids learned better [students brought less playground problems into the classroom]. Now aides come to me for help with problems."

Teachers differ about whether the Elkin administration values their input to improving the school. One teacher said, "The leaders encourage us to look at new ways of doing things. They are always sending out information for in-services and workshops to attend." Another teacher said, "I have a bias here, I think there is a 'we against them' attitude [among teachers].... I [her personal feeling] don't feel threatened and can say what is in my heart."

Skyland

A split-grade-level teacher said, "The big thing is if people don't respect your professional judgment. If they do not respect you, where is your power as a professional? I wish people trusted us more." Another teacher used an analogy to explain her position. "If you needed surgery you would not go to a doctor that used the methods from the 50s and 60s. If you did, people would think you were crazy. But parents want their children taught in the same manner as they were taught.... People have all gone to school. They are not all doctors. Maybe that is the difference. Or maybe it is fear of something new."

Teachers are concerned that the new Skyland board members will restrict their ability to make decisions in the classroom. A teacher said, "Businesses are telling us we need people who can cooperate with others. [They new board members] want kids in rows doing worksheets. That's not how you teach cooperation." A special education teacher said, "The [conservative] candidates stated what they wanted the school to do, but it is stifling the district. They are from the traditional families and don't realize we don't have that type of student population now."

A new board member questioned about the teachers' comments said, "That is not what the [conservative] candidates wanted. They wanted improvements based on tests showing [conservative candidates were concerned that recent and planned instructional changes would not result in improved student learning] that the changes improved instruction. So the fear was not based on what... we're about." An old board member said, "People get so single-minded about the roles of schools, they cannot imagine any change in that."

Teachers perceive that they can be involved in the decision-making process both individually and as a staff. A teacher explained group decision-making: "Everyone is a leader.... We work as a team in the school. We can all advance items on the agenda. There is time for everyone to be heard. We meet together to share." A specialty teacher said, "I am a member of the leadership team.... One of the board members wanted the teacher involved.... We talked about removing barriers that prevent teachers from improving." Other teachers reported having flexibility to teach the way they wanted to. A teacher said, "I spend most of my time in math." She explained how she integrates other subjects with math. Another teacher talked about integrating reading with other subjects.

Individual Acceptance

Teachers reject or accept change based on their definition of "good education" supported by their vision of a good classroom. "Individual acceptance," is a separate variable, independent of and more personal than "being valued in decision-making." The impact of teacher acceptance is often undervalued. A teacher in Dryden said, "From a self-preservation issue teachers become comfortable. When change occurs or needs to occur the teacher feels threatened...." A teacher in Elkin said, "We have done this for 20 years and it worked for me.... Why change?" A teacher in Skyland said, "People, some people, like the status quo. They learn that way, in that way they become comfortable."

Data suggest that teachers may have good reasons for their positions. Each school implemented new programs, and in each case the teachers used the political system to ensure that the new programs were dropped or modified so that the teachers could maintain their visions. This suggests that teachers feel safe when they can carry out programs that they believe are good for children and that present a good image.

Dryden

An example of the importance of individual vision for accepting or rejecting change was found in Dryden's attempt to mandate that teachers use a program called outcome-based education (OBE). Teachers divided in their support for OBE. One teacher claimed it is better. She said, "There are tests to measure the outcomes and standardized tests." When questioned about the test, she did not add to her response. Another teacher said, "I support OBE," but she could not explain why. A second-grade teacher expressed strong opposition to OBE. "We had an excellent program in math and science. OBE is inferior to what we had. OBE wastes a lot of time. We used to do multiplication in second grade; now we're told not to do that." Another second-grade teacher said, "I don't recall reading that OBE is better, but I don't know of any studies." She claimed that changes were being forced on teachers who did not know whether the new programs represented an improvement. When the researcher returned in the fall, he found that OBE was no longer a priority with the administration.

Elkin

Teachers who supported changing the instructional method to whole language perceived that they had input into the decision. One teacher said, "Lower elementary had been going to a lot of workshops and were sold on it." Another confirmed this: "We had a lot of in-services on it.... It began gradually in bits and pieces during a year or two. Then we were ready." The teachers involved in the in-service felt good about the change and valued the opportunity they had been given. Other teachers said, "The change was mandated from above." They opposed the change and saw the trained teachers as aligned with the administration. A teacher who did not support the change to whole language said, "Basically, we were told we were to do some form of whole language.... It was top-down management."

Elkin teachers support or reject change based on their perception of "good education". A teacher said, "In 16 years of teaching, I have found [this school] to be the best school I have ever worked at. [Teachers] want power in decision-making, but it is a kid-centered school [teachers are focused on students]. What you will likely see is not enough staff, not enough money, and not enough time [support for a kid-centered school]." Other teachers confirmed that they like working in this school, but their acceptance of change varied. One said, "There are people there that want to improve in my opinion.... Schools that do a poor job are not interested in change." Some teachers supported the need for change, but raised the questions of how and when. A teacher said, "We need flexibility in how we treat kids in different classes.... We need to be able to make changes early and quickly. We need innovative programs."

Teachers recognize there are differences of opinion about change. A teacher said, "We talk about it, but some want a textbook and don't want total hands-on, others like the other end of the spectrum." Another teacher said, "We have done this for 20 years and it worked for me and my children, why change? Teaching is a struggle between parents, community, and the teachers due to rapid change and a preconceived nature of education.... Where administration and parents make the mistake is by stating, 'You will do it this way.' This places the teacher on the defensive before the subject of change is talked about or had an opportunity for study."

Skyland

Skyland teachers, like those in Elkin, support or reject change based on their definition of a good education. A teacher said, "People, some people, like the status quo. They learn that way, in that way, they become comfortable, and don't want to change." An administrator said, "We need to teach with methods that are the latest. This is threatening to veteran staff members. That is the way they were taught to teach and that is the way they have taught for 25 years." A teacher disagreed: "I used to believe older teachers did not want to change. I don't believe that anymore."

Observations indicate that three teachers, Sam S1, Renee S2, and Vickie S7, in the school do not support the rapid changes in the district. Two are specialty teachers unaffected by methods used in the classrooms. The third, Sam S1, has a special program that she protects. In addition to these teachers, Dawn S3 supports change so long as her specialized program remains unaffected.

Trust in Administrative Leadership

Teachers base their trust in administration on the degree to which the administration protects and supports them. Teachers' inclination to distrust relates to three factors: contract administration, covert activities, and blaming of teachers. Leadership that uses any one or a combination of these factors can disrupt or support the teachers' ability to achieve their visions, by enhancing or reducing the rank of individuals or groups in the system.

The following examples of contract administration illustrate this process. In Dryden, teachers reported that the administration had acted unfairly when the staff was moved; also, suspension (fairly or unfairly) reduced the teacher's status and affected the social structure. In Elkin, teachers believed the principal had violated the contract when transferring a teacher. However, the transfer itself appeared not to be the issue. In Skyland, teachers were happy with the current administration, which supported them, but were concerned that changes on the board would reduce the level of support. In each case, teachers' reaction to administration was related to changes in the social structure affecting their ability to maintain their vision.

Dryden

The grade-level restructuring moved teachers against their wishes. Although the moves were in accordance with the management rights clauses in the contract agreement, teachers did not like the way the restructuring was done. They resented the lack of communication, often noting, "They didn't even ask for our input." Other comments included: "They did it behind everyone's back." "The lack of trust is just a feeling. Maybe they have created that by the way they did it." A teacher with more than 10 years in the district offered a variation on the theme of trust: "Educators have a general lack of trust in administration. Maybe it is a perception. Maybe the communication is not there." Teachers admit that they did not want to change, and fought the restructuring at scheduled public meetings and by sending letters of complaint. One teacher reported that she had spent hours drafting a letter and sharing it with other teachers.

The teachers' activities had no effect on the restructuring plan. Layoffs are common in the Dryden district. Following the restructuring, the district sent out several layoff notices and two teachers were not rehired for the subsequent school year. A board member said, "I do not see a problem with sending out layoff notices. It protects the district and people are usually rehired."

However, layoff notices affect teachers. A teacher who has received five layoff notices said, "I hate it. It was horrible. We just bought a home. It's scary and when someone takes something away that you have, it gets scary." Another teacher said, "There is always this feeling of insecurity of who is going to get layoff notices. Everyone feels insecure this time of year." From a different perspective, a teacher commented, "For me it doesn't really bother me. My income is not greatly affected, because my husband doesn't work in education."

Suspensions for misconduct also can cause teachers to distrust the administration. During the study, one suspension occurred. The staff lost work time while individuals discussed the case and its causes. Some teachers felt the administration acted responsibly; others argued it had acted in haste.

Teachers are cautious about discussing attempts by the administration to force staff to leave district employment. Three teachers claimed that teachers were moved to another school in the hope that they would retire. Two teachers claimed that a teacher was pressured to retire. The researcher looked for verification of these claims, but found none. Teachers continue to feel these undocumented claims were true.

Teachers are afraid of being blamed for events and situations outside of their control. The administration blamed one teacher for not controlling a student in his class who damaged school equipment. Two months later, administrators discovered that the damage was caused during after-school activities. Other teachers in the school discussed this case. In general, they do not want anyone to use their rooms, fearing that they will be blamed if something is broken.

Elkin

A teacher said, "Last spring a position was not posted correctly before hiring someone. Someone was moved before the posting." She did not like the person who was moved into the position. The principal denied that this had happened. He said the person had discussed the opening with him and he had explained the seniority situation. The person told staff members she was going to get the position before it was posted, but she was moved after the posting. The principal said, "I know the teachers do not see it that way."

One teacher reported that the principal used the PTO to achieve his objectives. She said the principal proposed a change in her program to the PTO, which voted to support his position. The principal did not see the incident in the same way, but changing the program did solve other problems for him. The principal also reported using peer pressure to resolve problems between teachers and other staff members. A teacher confirmed that a staff member had pressured her to change her class schedule.

Teachers reported that the principal blamed them for not completing a strategic plan for the building. A School Effectiveness Team (SET) involved teachers, parents, and administrators in solving problems and developing plans for improving the school. A teacher on the committee claimed that the principal blamed the teachers for stopping the progress of SET after the team suggested that the teaching staff donate their time over a weekend to develop a strategic plan. According to the teacher, her colleagues said, "We can't give any more time." Another member of the team said, "I think [the principal] took it personally." She said she heard him comment that "teachers are not committed." The principal says that two teachers stopped the process by claiming that the strategic plan would not allow them to make decisions in their classrooms. The researcher tried to discuss the principal's position with these two teachers, but both avoided his questioning.

Skyland

Teachers appreciate the administration's support of recent changes to the contract, which provide additional planning time during the day. They blamed the state for reducing planning time in the last contract, in order to cut positions.

Teachers did not report covert activities by the administration, and the researcher did not observe any such activity. But the conservative board members claim such incidents occur. One board member said, "Management is a problem. Our school uses the fear factor of management." Another board member said, "[The administration] had an active role encouraging fear among the teachers. They suggested to them these board members would be telling them what to do in their classrooms.... People who did not support their position were out on a limb." Both board members said they gathered this information from teachers who do not support the administration's positions and actions.

The old board members and the administration support the teachers' involvement in implementing the Strategic Plan; however, a conservative board member claimed that teachers did not follow the Strategic Plan and did not complete the assigned tasks. She said, "I was involved with the restructuring.... The board and the administration was telling the public this was a self-developed plan by the residents of the district.... I watched the way the plan was implemented through action committees.... The teams were not finished with their work and the teams were implementing things before they were finished or reporting their plan to the board for approval." She says that was one of her reasons for running for the board.

Hardworking Teachers

The educational culture encourages teachers to work hard, but teachers also have good reason to work hard. Teachers who spend time at school and associate with others of similar or higher status increase their status with teachers and parents. In addition to spending extra time on making advantageous personal/professional contacts, teachers work to maintain control of their classrooms in ways that protect their vision. They attempt to determine which students are placed in their rooms. This helps ensure that the classroom is well disciplined and presents a favorable image. They compete informally in decorating their rooms for parents, especially at the kindergarten and first-grade levels in each school. Teachers resist making changes in classroom management and methods of instruction unless the changes are compatible with their vision and enhance their image. Teachers make such intense efforts to control their work environment that they report being tired and in need of rest.

Dryden

Teachers work hard to control activities within their classrooms. The researcher regularly observed teachers before, during, and after school. Teachers were in their rooms 8½ to 9 hours a day. Before school started, they were working, preparing for the day, placing educational materials on desks, grading papers, organizing instructional activities, decorating the room, and/or preparing materials. When they were not in their rooms, they were engaged with other teachers, usually of the same grade level, developing plans for future activities such as assemblies, pictures, student awards, and field trips. The researcher asked whether these activities are similar each year. The teachers confirmed that they are; however, they do not have written procedures, so they discuss the schedules each year.

Three teachers spent time outside the school day finding and/or purchasing material for science activities with their own resources.

Teachers spend time in an attempt to control the class rosters by developing the lists themselves. A teacher stated the reason as, "so each of us gets an equal number of the troublemakers." Some teachers are upset when the administration honors parent requests because it unbalances the classes. Other teachers like having parent requests, because it means the parents support what they do in the classroom.

During observations, teachers complained about how tired they were. The school observation was conducted near spring break. Absenteeism had risen in the previous 2 weeks: Two teachers had doctor's appointments and two had bad colds. During an interview, a teacher with 25 years in the district voiced an angry opinion: "We need that [spring] break to get rested up for the remainder of the year. A board member was hard-nosed during negotiations to drop the breaks." The secretary responded to a question about high absenteeism before break, "This year [there] has been more."

According to a first-grade teacher, rest time is necessary during the school day. "You need a half-hour during the day [at lunch] for sanity." She explained that she can gain her strength back for the afternoon during this time. This individual eats in her room, listening to the radio. When she finishes with lunch, she sets up the room for the afternoon.

Teachers often complained about being pulled out of their classroom for training, meetings, and/or interviews. The complaints centered on preparing for substitutes and on not being with their kids. In general, teachers claim that the amount of in-service training has decreased and the district is slowing down the change process. This pleased them. Several teachers said, "I do not want to be gone from my kids any longer than needed."

Elkin

Teachers in Elkin work hard to control activities within their classrooms. Teachers were observed arriving at school earlier than 7:00 AM, an hour before they were scheduled to work. During this time, most teachers were in their rooms working, except for brief stops in the lounge for coffee. They placed educational materials on the desks, graded papers, organized activities, decorated the room, and/or prepared materials. Occasionally they would leave the room to coordinate activities with other teachers at the same grade level. Three teachers socialized in the lounge for 10 minutes before the students arrived. When school started each day, the students were working within seconds.

Yet, special activities seemed to lack coordination. Although groups of teachers would have plans, they were uncoordinated. Teachers with informal leadership roles would make contact with the principal to coordinate schoolwide programs.

Changes in the classroom affect these teachers' sense of control. A teacher with 25 years in the school said, "I developed an ulcer, due to the added stresses worrying about having a textbook." Other teachers reported stress because they did not know how closely they had to follow the textbook. All of these teachers reported spending time selecting a textbook that would support teaching whole language. A teacher commented, "Teachers want to do a good job, but the time commitment and planning cause them to stay in their classrooms and do what is comfortable."

Teachers talked about problems with students in their classes while in the lounge, but they were not observed attempting to change or preset class lists. Only one teacher commented on parent requests. She, Kathy El, said, "I usually get the most parent requests in the school, but I always ask for the low students to be placed in my room." The principal verified that this teacher does get the most requests and added, "Parent requests are pretty balanced and do not cause much of a problem." Other teachers did not seem concerned about parent requests.

Teachers report fatigue from long work hours that affect their performance in the classroom. A teacher with more than 25 years in the district said, "The one thing that prevents me from improving is the lack of energy to become involved. I just get tired out from all of the committee meetings." This teacher volunteers for committees that have decision-making power. Other teachers also reported being tired by attending meetings. One said, "We wanted a say, but it takes so much time on committees it tires me out for teaching."

Elkin's training and/or work assignments are held during the school day. Teachers report concern about being out of their classrooms, but they want time during the school day for planning. One teacher said, "So many of us would like the time to teach. At times we would like to tell administration to go away and let us teach." She reported being busy all of the time with meetings, conferences, in-services, and workshops, and said, "This takes me out of the classroom and away from preparing for class the next day. The problem is you are torn, many of the things do seem valuable." Another teacher said, "Responsibilities in the district take teachers out of the classroom." Teachers believe planning time is important, but have a conflict between planning and being in the classroom.

Skyland

Teachers work hard to control the activities in their classrooms. Before the school year began, teachers decorated their rooms and the halls, arranged the desks and placed the students' names on them, and produced or organized instructional materials. One teacher said, "The teachers here all come in 2 weeks prior to school." Another teacher described the staff: "I think they work well together. They are all a bunch of workaholics, very devoted, very professional."

During the school year, teachers started arriving at school at 6:30 AM. All but two were in the building by 7:45 AM. Before the children arrived, teachers worked in their rooms placing material on the students' desks, grading papers, and decorating the room or hall, or met in groups with others who teach the same grade. One morning, the researcher met a teacher in the parking lot at 6:50, and commented on her early arrival. She said, "This is the only free time I have. I leave the house while my husband and baby are still sleeping. At four o'clock (PM), I pick [the baby] up and it does not stop." This teacher is active in committee work in the evening.

Teachers worked as teams to develop class lists, but they are concerned about having children of difficult parents in their rooms. When a teacher was asked if she taught any students whose parents came into the school, she said, "I have been lucky so far. All the parents I have dealt with have been good. This year may be different." She explained that a mother from the conservative group had called to push her point of view. In the previous year, the teacher said, this parent had called the parents of other children in her room. She said, "This has placed a lot of doubts in other parents' minds."

The principal said the school honors parent requests for placement. "We do not get many, but they are evenly spread. So it is not a problem."

A teacher said, "Teachers that come here from other schools say they have their summers free. Here that does not happen. It always seems there is something new to learn." The teacher claimed there is no time to rest and get ready for the next year. Another teacher said, "You feel lucky to be in an innovative district, but it makes you feel inadequate and worn out."

Teachers are given time during the school day for planning. At one grade level, teachers had planning time each of 3 days during a single week. One day, substitutes taught the classes while teachers planned a large-group activity. Subs were hired for an additional half-day for CTC (the ill-defined activity discussed in Chapter 6). The week also included an early release day. The researcher asked a teacher how she felt about being out of class so often. She said, "The work has taken me out of my class, but it is important." Another teacher said, "We need the time to plan; we could use more."

Poor Teacher

This judgment is the most insidious of all of the constructs and variables that affect teachers' behaviors. Teachers, administrators, parents, and others such as community members use this key sanction to push out those who do not or cannot conform to the values and norms of the social structure. The data indicate that individuals' real or perceived images may be used to discredit them, merely because they do not fit the generally accepted culture or vision. Teachers protect themselves by aligning with powerful teachers, building their own status, or moving outside the system and becoming silent. In all three schools, teachers feared being labeled poor teachers and took action to protect themselves against that label.

Dryden

Teachers. Teachers generally do make negative comments about other teachers based on their perceptions of how they teach. A teacher with more than 25 years in the district said, "I think it is not fair, but it is usually a group of teachers that gets down on one teacher and [the group will] disregard what [that teacher has] learned. I have seen it happen many times." During observations, one group of teachers did not listen to or support a particular individual during the group's meeting. Later, responding to interview questions, these teachers used this person as an example of a poor teacher. The teachers based their comments on their own personal perceptions, but the researcher found classroom evidence that contradicted these perceptions. A certified support teacher who taught in this teacher's room defended her, saying, "They base their comments on misperception." She supported her comments with examples of effective teaching.

Teachers made negative comments based on their own beliefs. For example, a common comment was, "Some teachers are only here for the paychecks." Teachers who made comments like this were very active in committee work and/or close to the administration.

Administration. A teacher with more than 25 years in the district offered an example of a situation in which the administration did not support teachers. She claimed that the administration made negative comments about teachers who ran a "loose classroom," one in which discipline and instruction were not rigid. According to her, the administration openly made negative comments about the teachers. She said, "I received the students out of these rooms and found the kids had learned and the kids remember these teachers." When administrators were asked about teachers with loosely run classrooms or poor discipline, they would not comment. During observations of classroom performance, administrators did make comments about teachers, both positive and negative.

Parents. Teachers fears that parents will accuse them of being poor teachers are based both on past and present conflicts with parents and also on what they perceive has happened to other teachers. Although they report that most conflicts with parents are resolved, they fear that parents will gossip, causing other parents to see them as poor teachers. Two teachers reported that a group of parents planned to "create a problem for a teacher," and this led to a suspension. This incident was not verified.

Others. Two teachers reported feeling uncomfortable working with the Department of Social Services. They did not feel Social Services believed them, and perceived Social Services as not respecting confidentiality. Both teachers were forced to testify against parents in court. The teachers believed their interactions with Social Services reduced trust in their relations with other parents. However, both teachers reported having the support of parents of current students. Other teachers reacted to this incident by refusing to call Social Services themselves. One teacher pressured the administrator to call and report a case of neglect. She said, "I am not being hauled into court." Other teachers claimed to have no feelings about Social Services and to have had no contact with them.

Elkin

Teachers. Teachers make negative comments about other teachers based on their perceptions. A teacher with work experience outside of education said, "Teachers need to do other things before teaching or you don't see the whole picture." She feels teachers should spend the summer working in other fields rather than teaching summer school. Another teacher said, "I am noticing more [now,] teachers seem to be a lot less focused on what student needs are." Other teachers were specific about individual teachers' abilities. A teacher commented, "A particular teacher, I don't know how they got through college. It's like working with one of my students."

Teachers sometimes defend other teachers or negate past problems. A teacher with more than 10 years' experience said, "I used to think old teachers did not want to change. I don't believe that so much anymore. Change is harder for some people more than others; therefore, it is not an age thing."

One teacher, who was no longer at the school, was seldom mentioned. This individual was said to have caused other teachers to look bad, and current teachers preferred to avoid the subject. One teacher said, "A few staff members thought the person was harsh. I saw [the former teacher] with kids and they were always good with them. The problem started from one parent."

Administration. The administrator was happy that three teachers had retired. He said, "Two would not respond to improvement efforts. One was starting to be a good teacher.... One teacher told the newspaper, 'What I will miss is the conversations in the teachers lounge.'... That tells you something about the profession." A board member said, "Ten percent of the teachers are poor teachers."

Parents. One teacher raised the issue of parents who did not support her program, but she blamed the administration for causing the problem. This teacher developed a working relationship with the parent after a problem arose and was resolved.

During school registration, three parents spoke informally with the re-searcher. One parent said, "In the past we had a poor teacher for [a particular program].... [A different teacher] does a great job with her kids. She knows how to motivate them." While registration continued, another parent complained about the school psychologist. She said, "He looked at me like I was nuts. I told him that is the way it is going to be.... I am not having my child in that room." Later in the conversation, another parent was speaking with the parent who complained about the school psychologist. About another teacher, the first parent said, "I don't know why they let her be a [level] grade teacher." Three parents continued to talk about poor teachers they had in elementary school. Using them as a standard, the parents spoke favorably of two current teachers.

Others. Teachers did not report problems with community agencies, even when asked. They did believe the community's newspaper was critical about teachers and low test scores.

Skyland

Teachers. Teachers generally did not criticize others directly, but they did talk about other teachers. In the lounge, two teachers discussed a colleague. One said, "[So-and-so] does what she wants. She cannot handle more than one thing at once and cannot learn anything." The other said, "[So-and-so's] work load is only...kids. What does she do with her time?" Another teacher told a story about a specialty teacher. "This teacher did not have the best personal habits. She ate food during class and was not always in the building in the morning on time. The kids love to go to her class and the students did learn. Teachers' complaints about her personal habits and the time she arrived at school caused her problems. The ... teacher left the school because of the pressure." (Twice during this story, the teacher switched the title of the teacher to her own. This led the researcher to wonder if she has been talking about herself.)

A teacher with 20 years in the district claimed that teachers view criticism as a personal attack and backed up his comment with a story about phonics: "The [level] grade team noticed a problem in reading. The students were having difficulty in decoding words, and difficulty progressing. The issue was raised with the [lower grade level] and [grade level] teachers. The [level] grade team found there had been a reduction in teaching phonics in the earlier grades. We asked if they would move back to teaching more phonics. The end result was the [lower level] grade teachers felt like they were being told they were doing something wrong. They felt bad, because they were being criticized for not doing their job. The [level] grade teacher wanted some help, not to put down anyone. We did not do it again." He concluded his story by saying, "You know people don't like to be criticized, but we did not know why this problem had occurred in the first place. This is a dilemma in improving student learning."

Administration. Teachers did not report that the Skyland administration made negative comments about teachers. The administration was upset that a few teachers backed the conservative faction in the community, but generally the administrator supported teachers whom he viewed as working toward improving the school.

Parents. A teacher reported that a parent had attacked her for using poor teaching methods. The teacher was afraid of the parents and asked not to be quoted. The superintendent told a story about conservative parents who attacked the methods a teacher used to teach a particular subject. The students learned the material, but the parents insisted that the teacher return to the old method. Even though the teacher demonstrated that his method produced results, he left the district. The superintendent said the teacher felt he would always be labelled and targeted by conservative parents in the district.

Others. Teachers reported that, during the previous election, negative comments were made about certain teachers. A teacher said, "These poor teachers were talked about by the group [conservatives in the community]...[who] and tried to drive a wedge between the administration and teachers." Articles in the local newspaper reported that teachers who did not teach in a traditional manner had been singled out and named.

SUMMARY

Examples given in each general category—social structure, support system, competition, being valued in decision-making, individual acceptance, trust in administrative leadership, hardworking teachers, and label of a poor teacher—demonstrate that these eight factors within the internal environment culture are linked to other dimensions. The social structures are closely linked and similar to the political power structure of the communities. This structure between and within the external and internal environment provides teachers with a personal and professional support system. Maintaining and strengthening the social structure, and competing for material and personal rewards, builds status that increases the teachers' perceptions of their value in decision-making. When individuals' abilities or beliefs threaten the social structure, they are forced either to conform or to leave the schools. Teachers' trust in leadership seems closely linked to how the formal leader threatens or protects the social structure. Teachers work hard to protect what they value. They expend a large amount of energy to ensure that their vision of a good classroom is not violated and to protect themselves from being labeled a poor teacher.

The external and internal cultures of each school district appear to be in constant struggle, each trying to protect its vision of a good school or classroom. External forces (community members, parents, students, state and national government officials) continuously interact with the internal culture (all paid and unpaid employees of the school district). Unfortunately, the struggle keeps the system in constant imbalance, and increases the stranglehold on the schools. The vision promoted by the external culture encourages the development of a safe, closed internal culture that protects the teachers' visions of a classroom. As a consequence, the system resists innovation and avoids the label "poor teacher."

COMMENT

Mackey and Mackey (1992) argue that barriers to change are inherent in a school's culture. These barriers include competition, lack of common purpose, and too few personal relationships. Other authors add personal beliefs about the value of an innovation (Lezotte, 1992a; Glasser, 1990a; Purkey and Smith, 1985). This study confirms these findings, and also adds other factors to the list of barriers. Teachers' dedication to meeting their own expectations of a good teacher and protecting themselves is exhausting. Teachers need to feel valued. They need personal and professional support systems that validate their work as teachers. Teachers mistrust administrative actions that create changes in the social rank of members in the culture. Teachers fear being sanctioned by being labeled a poor teacher.

CHAPTER 8

Leadership

INTRODUCTION

Two types of leadership affect school districts, schools, and the classroom: formal and informal. Formal leaders are sanctioned through election or appointment. Informal leaders develop power through their ability to give recognition, withhold rewards, or carry out sanctions. The sociograms of school social structures in Dryden, Elkin, and Skyland provide excellent examples of informal leadership.

Both formal and informal leaders are powerful influences on the cultures of the external and internal environments, as they attempt to protect their visions of good schools and classrooms. In an ethical society, informal leadership has as much responsibility as formal leadership to improve student learning. Informal and formal leaders must work hand in hand against all factors that could strangle school improvements.

Some people have argued that all organizational activities begin and end with leadership; that without formal or informal leadership, nothing happens within the organization. But we can also think of individuals as "leaders unto themselves." According to Glasser (1984), individuals will only do what is aligned with "pictures in their album." This means that individuals can choose to lead themselves. Individual leadership can be as simple as leading oneself to work, or as complex as developing and implementing innovations with others. In any case, leadership is the critical factor that drives an organization.

Three general concepts—top-down management, leadership instability, and informal leadership—affect school improvement in the leadership dimension. Top-down management promotes the political system regardless of whether the leadership is formal (for example, the board of education or any administrator) or informal (for example, the social structure of the teachers' culture). Top-down management can and does control, give or withhold support, and provides or withholds rewards; such actions seem to promote the political structure and directly or indirectly block improvement. The instability of formal leadership can create an opportunity for informal leadership to lose, assume, or maintain control over their vision. This chapter examines each of these factors.

During the data collection process, the variables of top-down management and informal leadership were separated. In presenting the findings, top-down management forms a general category with formal and informal leadership as subvariables.

LEADERSHIP DIMENSION

Top-Down Management

Formal leadership's ability to force change is grounded in legislated laws that delegate authority. This top-down authority allows an administration to carry out plans for change without considering its effects on teachers. When management forces a change, it angers teachers because they have no control and are placed at risk by administrative action. Intentional or not, the actions of formal leadership promote the paradox. Changes intended to bring improvement will strangle the desired changes, if the imposed change goes against the teachers' visions.

Formal leadership can threaten a teacher's vision in several ways: by controlling activities or resources that support the teacher, or by providing unequal support to teachers as rewards and sanctions. The study revealed several examples of unequal support: providing or withholding resources for new or old programs; forcing some teachers to use methods not aligned with their visions, while permitting others to teach as they wished; and allowing or discontinuing work projects. All of these examples affect the teachers' status. Teachers have learned that the higher their status is with administrators, the more rewards they reap; this promotes the paradox.

Teachers counteract the controls of formal leadership through their informal leadership structure. The teachers who lead the informal structure gain power through their own use of rewards and sanctions. For teachers to effectively use their informal power, they must continually build support to control the formal leadership, as well as parents, community members, and agencies outside the school organization.

The three school systems studied illustrate these observations in three different ways.

Dryden

The restructuring caused teachers to feel a loss of control. One teacher said, "If we could have been placed in [the particular school] and built on the program and continued, we would be teaching and have control of what we were doing."

She explained that she had worked closely with the principal and had her support, but both had been moved. Another teacher was angry that her colleagues had no control over the board decision to restructure. She said, "Board members have no idea about what teaching is all about." She claims that the change caused her to lose control of her personal instructional program.

Equipment for preparing instructional materials was kept in the lounge. A teacher came in, looked at the researcher, and said, "We cannot copy anything on construction paper. We needed that spirit duplicator; however, the head of maintenance said we could not have flammable fluids in the school. Now we have to trace things on construction paper. That uses your time."

Two teachers were upset with the administration when they perceived that administrators withdrew support from their team approach to planning. Both teachers claimed that the principal had formerly supported and praised their program. One said, "We had each other to...balance each other out personally and professionally.... We were very upset that we were broken up, because we had done everything [the administration] wanted us to do."

When the administration removed teachers from projects, the teachers also lost important intangible rewards. A team of paid teachers worked a whole summer on OBE (outcome-based education) for math. During the restructuring, members of the team were moved to other schools and grade levels. One teacher said, "We all sat down and cried when we found out that they were moving us. It was just taken away. We had a good program that we worked hard on. Now no one is doing it.... Basically, the administration didn't appreciate all that work, and it was work." The researcher probed further to determine what she valued for rewards: "You were paid for the work, so what was the problem?" The teacher said, "You don't understand, we did what they asked, then we were not allowed due to.... We were looking at putting the information together and telling other districts about it." Other teachers reported similar feelings that the restructuring had taken away the rewards inherent in working on specific programs.

During the restructuring a teacher was moved to a different grade level in which she had a certification the district needed. After the move, she worked with established teachers who had been teaching for some time at her new grade level. She said, "I had a sense of accomplishment...[before] I came to [the new grade level]. Now I am surrounded by three people [established and respected teachers] that are very accomplished and I feel very inadequate."

Elkin

Teachers appear to control the decision-making process within the Elkin school. Leadership makes decisions based on the perceived support of others. The teachers seem to determine whether the district should purchase new language textbooks. Both the administration and a teacher suggested that teachers had persuaded the superintendent and curriculum director to purchase texts that would allow individual teachers to use instructional methods they preferred.

Teachers perceived they had lost the support of central administration when they told teachers to select a textbook for whole language; however, teachers felt they had gained support from the building principal. A teacher with more than 25 years in the district said, "[The principal] said I do a good job with the students and I did not have to use the textbook, only teach what the book covered." The principal rejoined, "I did not say she did not have to use the textbook. I said she could supplement materials." However, the teaching staff believed they had only to follow the intent of the textbook, and could use it or not as they wished.

The administration established a committee system to give teachers more say in the decision-making process. Teachers viewed this as an opportunity to have more input. For example, one teacher said, "We used to complain about not being heard, that is why we have committees, for a voice; however, sometimes we make a recommendation that the administration does not follow." As an example, she said a committee had recommended not having formal report cards, but "the administration would not let [us] do that." Another teacher believed this administrative decision protected the district. "Things would be easier if the school could make its decisions," she said, "but the realization is some things need to be districtwide."

Teachers did not say they felt unrewarded when administrators overruled their decisions, but commented, "We're not being treated as professionals."

Skyland

The strategic plan and current governance policy ensures that Skyland teachers have decision-making power. An administrator says that pressure from the community threatens the teachers' power. "[Teachers] now defend the [old strategic] plan by saying, [with this plan] 'You don't tell me that I cannot do cooperative learning. Don't tell me I cannot do whole language. Don't tell me I cannot do an innovation." A teacher said, "We have tried to move from top-down management to site-based management [SBM]. We are trying to be part of the process.... We had top-down management by administration; now we're looking at top-down management from parents." Another teacher said, "Faculty councils were excited that they could do what they wanted." A specialty teacher said, "[Community members] do not want SBM; they do not want schools doing their own thing. It is a power issue. They want teachers to be more responsive to their way.... The community wants top-down management."

Teachers say that the current method of decision-making supports them personally and professionally. One teacher said, "I see it differently. Some teachers see top-down [management] from the board and the community. I see SBM as the administration, two board members, parents, teachers as a team.

SBM is much safer for me, because if I had a parent complaint or a problem with the report card I could say I had broad-based support. Then it would validate the decision."

Teachers of specialty programs are concerned that changes on the board threaten their programs. One specialty teacher noted that a new board member had voted against hiring an additional teacher to free her to teach the specialty program. Split-grade-level teachers are concerned that the board will force them to teach classes with one grade level. The researcher asked a split-grade-level teacher why this concerned her. She explained, "[Now] I can start teaching the first day of school. I know where half of the kids are at and I know half of the parents." Because parents select the split-grade-level format for their children, last year's parents already know and support her, and she only has to be concerned with meeting the parents of the new children.

Teachers perceive as rewarding the current process used to develop and implement changes in the school district. They believe that the administration wants to protect this system, but new board members threaten the process that rewards teachers for implementing change.

Instability

The instability of formal leadership appears to threaten teachers' control, but teachers can also use instability to protect their visions. Instability in formal leadership is created by change in leadership personnel or change in the leadership's ability to act.

In each subject school, the boards of education were unstable. This led to varied results.

In Dryden, teachers used the board's instability to block administration actions to stabilize the culture after the restructuring. Teachers were concerned that administrators would continue to create changes that threatened the teachers' culture. In Elkin, powerful teachers, aligned with the "old guard," created instability in the board's decision-making process, by helping elect a board member aligned with their vision. The instability worked to the powerful teachers' advantage by blocking the strategic plan. The data suggest that the strategic plan provided for decision-making power at the committee level. This prevent powerful teachers from controlling plans for improvement and threatened the power of the "old guard."

In Skyland, the instability of the board's membership threatened teachers' part in controlling of the decision-making process. Teachers had gained control of the administration and members of the board of education. However, their ability to control changed when a substantial number of people in the community became concerned that the new curriculum was not aligned with their values or expectations of student learning. This caused teachers to focus on maintaining control; they feared the new board members would determine what they did in their classrooms.

Instability in the administrative leadership promotes teachers to maintain their personal vision. One teacher said, "Administration moves on and we are still here." Her comment reflects the sentiments of other teachers, who say that new leaders always try to introduce their own "pet programs." Teachers in each school said that they had followed their administration's programs in the past, but found that new programs were introduced when leadership changed.

Despite the obvious power of administrative leaders, administrators could not act on their own in any of the schools. This circumstance created fear among teachers with little power, because in each school, the powerful teachers used the powerlessness of administration to their advantage. And administrators used favoritism to protect their own position. But administrative favors increased the status of some teachers, and demonstrated to others that they could use power to gain what they needed to achieve their own visions.

Dryden

Board of Education. The board of education's actions and beliefs were unstable; this concerned teachers both personally and professionally. Teachers were uncomfortable with changes in the board's membership and its directions for action. A teacher said, "A new school board member was elected on the grounds to change the school back to the way it was." Another teacher said, "The board member wanted a report on all the extra activities the kids had when the teachers should be teaching. She thought it was a waste of tax dollars." The principal verified the detrimental effect of the board member's request, reporting that this teacher had asked, "Is it OK to give rewards for good behavior such as movies or field trips that are not part of the instructional program?" The principal approved the activity and explained to the researcher, "Canceling extra activities took the teacher's power away to support the learning in her room."

The researcher interviewed two Dryden board members to verify these reports. The board members did not recall the stories. One said, "The board drove fear into the organization the last 3 years, more than anytime [earlier] while I was on the board. I got tired of being good to people and having it thrown back in my face. We got threatened by people [who were] not doing their job." The other member said, "Things are taken out of context and the teachers will not let them go. This causes the board not to have open discussions during the board meetings. Once the damage is done it [fallout from the damage] takes away from education." He states he would like more input, but other board members do not feel that way. However, both members interviewed believe they should not be involved with the day-to-day operation of the school district; the administration's job is to run the district.

Board instability has produced instability in the administrative staff. The district has a history of forcefully removing administrators. One board member claims that in the past, the board of education did not control the district. The two most recent superintendents were hired to regain administrative control. The board member said, "[The former superintendent] took back the control of the school and the teachers did not like that. Now someone was telling them to write curriculum and have it coordinated. The board knew there was a problem and wanted the changes to happen." Both board members reported that pressure from teachers and the community forced the board to change administrators.

Changing Leadership. A teacher with 25 years in the Dryden district said, "I am frustrated about the constant change in administration. I have had six or seven principals, each with a different perception of education. They [the administration] look at the whole. I look at it as a tunnel. My classroom." Another veteran teacher said, "Administration comes and goes. Teachers are asked to change direction and they work hard on the change. Then new administration changes direction and we start something different. Teachers then feel, why do we have to put the effort in, it's going to change again anyway."

Powerlessness. A special education teacher observed that the current superintendent/principal has no power. She said, "[The teachers] have a lack of leadership; they don't have any support. It is a dysfunctional school with the heroes and scapegoats.... The guy is so ineffective [the teachers] are free to do whatever they want to do. They are very independent." A board member confirmed these comments, saying, "[The superintendent/principal] had control of the district, then lost it." The board member believed the superintendent/principal was going in the right direction, but implementation of new programs was failing. So the board did not renew his contract. This also happened to the last two superintendents.

Administration Protecting Themselves. The superintendent/principal claims his problems started when the administrative team "blinked" (backed away from the planned direction), giving the teachers control. He said, "This reinforced that the teaching staff did not trust the assistant superintendent." A teacher close to the administration said, "[The assistant superintendent] received the heat for the low test scores at the high school. The administration got together for protection and said, in effect, that one person will not be the fall guy." The former principal of the school claimed this was the result of an attack by a board member. She said the elementary school was working on improving math scores, but improvement had not started at the high school where the tests were taken. Shortly after this event, the board sent nonrenewal letters to the entire administrative staff. The researcher asked a board member to comment on the nonrenewals. He said, "I really did not see a problem with that when they knew it was to protect the board [from state spending controls] and they would be rehired." However, the assistant superintendent left the district and the superintendent resigned. A certified specialty teacher said, "Now we can change the schools back to the way they were." Her class schedule did not change after restructuring.

Favoritism. When leadership bends the rules, some see it as favoritism and others as resolving problems. For example, the teaching staff is split over the effects of honoring parent requests to place their child with a specific teacher. One group of teachers wants parent requests, because such requests establish a desirable mix of students in their classrooms. These teachers support the administration's informal honoring of requests. Other teachers believe the process disrupts the mix of students in the classroom. These teachers view the practice as favoritism. Leadership views the practice as resolving conflict with teachers and parents.

One teacher was angry about her history in the district. She complained that she had been moved twice, while a teacher with less seniority remained in her room. She said, "I am angry that nothing ever happens to her." The less senior teacher is close to the administration. Two other teachers confirmed this situation. One said, "I don't know anyone that will stand up to him. He handpicks his people." She would not name who was handpicked. Another teacher described the favored teacher by grade level and said, "She is found in the superintendent/principal office before meetings."

Elkin

Board of Education. The Elkin board of education's actions and beliefs cause teachers concern personally and professionally. A teacher said, "The board members are the powers that be [have absolute power] and they work together and have been the crux of a lot of the change." Another teacher said, "The board is always changing and they have to be responsible to the public." During the last two elections, the power on the board changed, when board members were elected from among the new members of the community. The researcher asked a new board member why she ran for the board. She said, "A board member asked me to run for the board. He said, 'You would be good.' He said he was open-minded and interested in kids' educational background. The board member believed I thought the same way he did. He claimed he needed more allies on the board. The votes were always a 3–2 split on everything."

The newest member of the board ran to control costs and problems with the administration. He said, "I am the 'no' vote on the board as far as salary. I feel a less-than-inflation raise is OK. Other people have taken it. They can suffer with it also.... I had a big problem with administration." He explained that he did not see the need for administrators, who make too much money.

The board members were asked whom they talk to before making decisions. The newest member of the board reported being very conservative. He said, "I talk to people in the community" and named individuals associated with the newspaper and businesspeople from the old, established families, the "old guard". The liberal board member who won the previous election reports talking to the PTO president, teacher Kathy E1, teachers influenced by Kathy E1, parents influenced by Marge E3, and the principal. She said, "I know when I try to make a decision I personalize it. If it's good for my kids, it is good for all kids."

A teacher reported that the board makes decisions based on whoever talks the loudest. Another teacher said, "As teachers we joke about it. If you have [a lot of loud] parents saying we don't want 25 in a classroom, that's when the change comes about." The board members interviewed had different ideas about how the school should function. The newest member said, "The board doesn't give enough mandates, [and] we are going to site-based management. I believe the board should grab back some of its power." The other board member said, "We should be out of the day-to-day operations and be more futuristic thinking." Both board members report split votes of 3–2 and 4–1. The superintendent confirmed that the board has great difficulty in passing policies. He said, "The board is very slow to pass policy the last 3 to 4 years.... We have some strong-minded individuals."

The new board member thinks he has caused the administration, including the superintendent and principals, to change. He said, "[The superintendent] is good at giving out information, but he is starting to become a sore loser." This board member criticized the superintendent for not achieving the goals of the strategic plan in a timely manner. The superintendent and principals responded that the need for board approval and the timing of the board meetings had made the time line so short that it could not be followed.

The board was blocked from making change or supporting the teachers' committee structure in decision-making that threatened the powerful teachers.

Changing Leadership. The administrative position in the district has changed gradually over the past 7 years, after previous administrators were pressured to leave. A teacher said, "We need them home grown." A 20-year teacher said of the former administrator, "He tried to initiate programs: tracking, cuts, and changes, but he was hired for that role. When they hired [the current superintendent] they did not want to make a change again [hire a person from outside the district]." She reported that after the previous superintendent left, many of his programs were carried out. Another teacher with 20 years in the district said, "We destroyed the last superintendent in 3 years. Now this person sells...[as a consultant]."

Powerlessness. The principal feels he cannot buck the "old guard." He believes if he does, the district will fire him. He was observed taking work direction from the office secretary. The principal claims she gained all of her power under the previous principal, who was never in the building, leaving the secretary and teachers free to do as they wished. At teachers' meetings the principal frequently said, "I will do it any way that you want it done." After one meeting he said, "It didn't make any difference to me; if they want to control it, that's OK." He told the researcher about an individual he did not want to hire. "I was told if I did not recommend her, they would go to the superintendent and the board. [She] was hired [by me]."

Administration Protecting Themselves. Two and three years ago, the administration supported the development of a strategic plan for the district and individual buildings. The plan included a wide range of committees established to set and implement guidelines and goals. In the last year, the process of setting goals and following the strategic plan has stopped. The principal said, "Everything was going fine until a couple of teachers blocked it." Both the principal and superintendent reported backing away from the plan to regroup, in response to changes on the board. Both want to retire from the district. The principal said, "We don't want to rock the boat too hard."

Favoritism. Elkin teachers did not report concerns about favoritism. One teacher said of the principal, "He listens to everyone." Another teacher agreed, "He is always willing to help and listen to what you have to say." The principal appeared to permit teachers to employ whatever good teaching strategy they requested unless it had financial impact or interfered with other activities.

Skyland

Board of Education. Teachers are concerned about the recent change in board membership, unsure what direction the Skyland board will take and how it will affect their professional careers. A teacher said, "Two years ago we had an ideal school board. They varied in their ideas and wanted accountability, but were concerned about improving the schools. They took their collars off and built a fence [gave teachers the ability to establish teaching activities without controls from outside of the school]. It was a dream come true. I need to know the goals and boundaries. The new boundaries are back to the leash [strong control over what teachers do]." Another teacher said, "We had the most progressive board anyone had ever had." The principal seconded this comment, and said of a particular board member, "He had a very liberal agenda and has a good understanding of what good education is."

Teachers fear the board agenda has changed. A teacher said, "One board member at the strategic planning meeting had talked about changing the mission statement and made this comment, 'I've been going to the truck stop and asking people what the school should be doing.' This board member apparently believes that the parents [or any committee member] should be able to totally tell what the teachers should teach. This is demeaning to the teachers." Another teacher said, "It is a battle of how they want the school board to be. It makes it hard for teachers." She mentioned a program the new board members want to eliminate. "The program has only 2 years in the district and they want to drop the program before it is determined if the program is effective."

The researcher asked the two new conservative board members why they had run for election. One member said, "There are three reasons.... Accountability...changes are based on some untested theories;...second...concerns of the methods, type of instruction, like whole language.... Third...the trust issue. We were lied to by the teachers and the administration in the changes the school was making." As an example, he said, the school had been asked whether it was implementing OBE. He claims that teachers and an administrator said "No" until they were shown to be lying. (The researcher found that the school personnel called OBE "cognitively guided instruction.")

The other new board member said, "The problem was not so much chaos...it was skirting dysfunction.... We were concerned that the educational structuring caused the schools to forget about student learning. They were more concerned about taking care of students than teaching them."

Changing Leadership. The people occupying the Skyland building principal's and superintendent's positions had changed within the 3 years prior to the study. One teacher reported, "I didn't like working for the former principal." Another teacher agreed, "The former principal was hard to work with." The current principal claims that the staff forced the former principal out, because the individual's management style was directive. The current superintendent was hired after the strategic plan had been developed. He said, "I was not here when it was developed. It was here when I got here and I did not have any ownership in it." An old board member said, "Good superintendents have two choices. One, to stay with the status quo and stay. Two, they can try to change the system and not care what happens to them personally. In other words they can create change, but work themselves out of the organization. That is the tragedy right now."

Powerlessness. The principal confirmed that she does not have power to control the teachers. The researcher asked the principal if either teacher Sam S1 or Dawn S3 could stop a specific program in the school. The principal paused, and then said, "I believe they could."

Administration Protecting Themselves. The Skyland community's split into two factions has caused the administration to proceed with caution. The superintendent and principal view their roles as advisory. The superintendent said, "Change and solutions come from the people of the district.... Every staff [member], administrator, community member, and parent all have a role...I see my role as giving them advice, clarifying the district's philosophy, and giving my opinion. That doesn't mean that is the way to go. It is going to be interesting with the new developments in the strategic plan."

The principal was observed conducting a teachers' meeting. She permitted the teachers to establish the agenda and control the discussion. When she was asked questions, she referred them to others, saying she could not respond because of the change in the governance policy, or because she needed additional information. An old board member said, "[The administrators] spend a lot of time justifying and rethinking where to go from here."

Favoritism. No Skyland administrator, teacher, or member of the support staff reported administrative favoritism, but the new board members reported specific incidents. One board member said, "They use this method to bring teachers into line. An example is administration giving individuals money outside of the base budget for materials, supplies, and in-service. The people that receive the money are supportive of the administration's position." The researcher's observations support this board member's comments. The administration supports teachers who implement favored innovations. These teachers have access to the administration, and are given time at meetings and in-services to promote their programs. Administrators also defended these teachers when questioned by the researcher.

INFORMAL LEADERSHIP

Informal leaders are individuals who have sufficient influence among group members to regulate behavior. They are individuals who have achieved a high social rank by their ability to give recognition, withhold reward, or carry out sanctions. Informal leaders attempt to influence the formal leadership by building support among those they lead, to block or support changes that enhance and/or maintain the system. These actions will protect their vision. Chapters 9, 10, and 11 consider results of these actions and how informal leadership uses influence.

Dryden

In regard to the district's restructuring planning, a member of the Dryden board of education said, "I think a lot of cliques keep stirring the pot even when [the pot] does not need [stirring]."

Under some circumstances, teachers would disagree. For example, the board members thought the district restructuring was completed, and the issue should be off everyone's agenda. Teachers should go with the board's decisions. Teachers did not share this opinion, and engaged in activities to return the district to its original structure. A special certified teacher was observed asking parents for their help in this effort. Support staff also wanted the school to return to the former grade levels. An aide said, "When they moved the upper grades out of the school, we lost some of our [the school's culture] sense of community."

As informal leaders, some Dryden teachers work actively to control the direction of committee work. The researcher attended a building committee meeting at which teachers Lori D1 and Lisa D2 were present. These teachers, working with the superintendent and head of maintenance, controlled the agenda to get what they wanted, such as improvements to their rooms (lowered ceilings and phones). After the meeting Lori D1 met with the superintendent to reinforce decisions made at the meeting. Another teacher, not on the committee, was angry about the outcome and said, "Why should we have the phones and drop the reading specialist and guidance counselor? All the parents want them [reading specialist and guidance counselor], but there's no money." The researcher asked other teachers whether people at the meeting controlled the administration, but they were not willing to give detailed information. A teacher said, "They seem to have power over the administration. They are…teachers full of enthusiasm, but have tunnel vision. They do not look at the whole school. They focus on what is good for one person."

Elkin

Teachers use school time to build a support system that allows them to function in a manner that they perceive as "good for kids." A specialty teacher reported talking to parents affected by an administrative decision, which forced her to use the gym rather than the stage for musical programs. She said, "We have a fine stage, but I don't agree. It does not have to be used to appease people when the school has outgrown that room." She believes that PTO support for her position will change the administration's decision. A special education teacher reported providing services to a child, outside the guidelines set by the administration. She said, "It kept the parents out of my face. Now [the student] is very happy with me…. We don't have any more problems with them."

Other teachers work closely with the PTO to build personal support as well as support for school activities, programs, and equipment. In discussions in the lounge, teachers suggested that if the PTO provided some of the money for an activity, it would occur. They reported having field trips turned down until the PTO agreed to fund all or part of the trip.

Teachers actively control decision-making at the school. Observing teachers' behaviors at school during one particular day, and attending an after-school teachers' meeting that day, indicated how two teachers planned to control a decision. Teacher Kathy E1 said to Kim E6, "You bring it up and I will support you." Both teachers talked to others about the decision during the day. When the issue was raised at the meeting, six teachers were vocal, and the principal concurred. Other teachers were intimidated and did not speak. After the meeting two of the teachers were angry. One said, "They railroaded it without discussion [I was not allowed to have input.]."

Skyland

Teachers actively build support systems that enable them to function in a manner they perceive as good for kids. At a teachers' meetings, individual teachers promoted their programs by explaining contests, talking about successes in the classroom, asking for help, and supporting other teachers' programs. They placed explanatory material in the lounge, sent home fliers with children, and placed displays in public areas to promote their programs. Teachers also met informally with board members or other members of the community to build support for their programs.

Skyland teachers attempted to control the decision-making process prior to formal and informal meetings within the school and school district. Before staff meetings, they talked about agenda items in the lounge and halls. When agenda items were presented at the meetings, teachers with informal power ensured their passage. For example, at one meeting, a schedule was presented to permit students to attend physical education, art, and music classes. Before the meeting, Vickie S7 met with Sam S1, Renee S2, and S8; Sam S1 met with S9. When the item was open for discussion at the meeting, Vickie S7 explained the plan. Immediately after she finished talking, first Renee S2, then Sam S1, and finally Dawn S3 verbally supported the plan, although they did not have the floor. S10 gained the floor and questioned the plan. Not one teacher responded. The principal asked for discussion, but the plan was accepted without comment. Similar processes occurred when teachers attempted to control district committee meetings discussing governance policy and mission statements.

Teachers who favored and opposed the innovations being carried out in the school held informal and secret meetings with board members and candidates before the last election. Both old and new board members confirmed that they had talked with teachers. One teacher explained, "I met with [the old board members], but did not help them write articles for the newspaper; other teachers did." Other teachers, questioned about their involvement in the campaign, refused to respond. For example, Sam S1 said, "I will pass on that." Both new board members confirmed that teachers had called them and set up secret meetings. These board members claimed that the teachers were afraid the administration would make it hard for them if their actions were discovered. They said that they had spoken with but would not name the five teachers. The researcher drew, from descriptions offered by both groups of board members, the impression that Sam S1 framed her innovative program in a manner that could be supported both by the old board members and by their conservative challengers.

SUMMARY/COMMENT

The literature makes numerous claims about how formal leadership can improve student learning. In addition, past studies suggest that leadership establish a constancy of purpose (Blankstein, 1993; Deming, 1993; Lezotte, 1992a) reflecting societies' needs through open dialogue (Audette and Algozzine, 1992). This study suggests that formal leadership is powerless to act separately from the school's informal organizational power structure. When formal leadership actions threaten the informal leadership's vision, the formal leaders will meet sanctions directed by the informal leaders. Then the top-down management structure contributes to keeping the organization the same, because it threatens the informal leadership's vision.

In all three schools, instability in leadership did not allow the development of a constancy of purpose. Skyland is a good example: Two groups of people worked hard, in good faith, to improve their school, resulting in instability of a vision for the school district. In all three schools, teachers and administration protect themselves from the risk of sanctions by either the formal or informal power structure. Observing leaderships' actions suggests that top-down leadership, formal or informal, leads to maintaining the status quo.

CHAPTER 9

Complete, Incomplete, and Thwarted Planning

INTRODUCTION

Strategies occur as a result of leadership attempts to change the organizational structure. This happens when leadership wants to produce different results and to balance the needs of the external and/or internal cultures. A strategy is a process, a formal or informal analysis and execution. People in either the external or internal environment use strategy to develop and implement a plan. The plan may maintain the status quo, or it may resolve a perceived or real problem.

Formal strategies are generally based on theoretical considerations by researchers who collect and interpret data, or on a written strategic plan describing a process that has produced (or is perceived to have produced) predictable results in the past. Usually, formal strategies such as strategic planning are employed by formal leadership. Informal strategies are based on "gut feeling" and on past experience. They are not written down, and activity is based on the intuitive feelings of individuals or groups.

Studies suggest that both formal and informal processes are involved in developing strategies for change or for maintaining the status quo. Formal and informal leadership strategies interact to enhance or protect the leaderships' visions. This chapter looks at the strategies used by our now-familiar three school systems to achieve their plans.

STRATEGY DIMENSION

As described in Chapter 4, leadership and strategy dimensions are closely linked. Leadership, formal or informal, develops strategies to balance external and internal forces so as to enhance or maintain their vision. Formal leadership strategies that carry out perceived improvements do not always generate a common vision among leadership groups. Nor does formal leadership always establish or follow guidelines for carrying out improvements. This permits teachers, administration, board members, parents, and the community to use their own power and influence in ways that reframe or block strategies intended to lead to overall school improvements.

Unclear Purpose

The formal leadership in each school used various formats for "strategic planning" to develop a mission for that school. Each school's administration assumed that if they involved the community in the plan's development, the outcome would be widely accepted by teachers, parents, and the community. However, special interest groups thwarted each plan.

In Dryden, the superintendent/principal used the strategic plan to convince the board to carry out innovations and to restructure the school district. However, formal leadership did not share the plan or provide a clear understanding of the district's direction. The teachers were not involved in the planning. They resented the changes, which altered the school's social structure and forced teachers to use instructional methods counter to their own visions. As the changes were implemented, teachers perceived that the superintendent/principal granted special favors to the few teachers he liked or feared. Teachers countered the superintendent/principal's action by attacking him in the community and at school. This rendered him powerless to complete the changes he had begun to implement. What did teachers learn? Changes last only as long as the leadership.

In Elkin, the administration used a complex system of committees and subcommittees to develop a districtwide strategic plan. The assumption was that involvement of many people would result in acceptance of the plan. Teachers appeared excited about their involvement. During the process of developing the district's mission and goal statements, the power was distributed throughout the system. However, this meant that powerful teachers were losing their influence. The system had taught these teachers that if they could control decision-making, they could protect their vision; therefore, they blocked completion of the plan. They increased the number of committees and subcommittees, making the system more complex; this blocked committees from implementing any plans they developed, or mired them in ongoing work. The powerful teachers also blocked any attempt to develop a clear mission by controlling the wording of the mission and goal statements.

In Skyland, too, the administration used a popular method that involved many people in developing a strategic plan, and assumed this would lead to wide acceptance of the school's mission. Teachers embraced the plan, along with more than 300 people who worked on several committees. They established a mission statement, essential learning outcomes, and a design to develop action plans. To communicate the mission statement and essential learning outcomes to everyone in the district, professional posters were printed and widely distributed. The plan was going well—until part of the community decided that the schools were moving away from the basics and were teaching "values." This emerging group claimed that teachers and administrators controlled the outcomes of the strategic plan by placing key people on the committees. Teachers and administrators denied the "accusation," but evidence suggested that the committees were comprised of people already involved with the school. Now two powerful factions were in a struggle to control and drastically modify the plan most teachers support. Teachers reported feeling that they were losing their ability to act as professionals. They did not precisely define what this meant, but they stated they were concerned about losing their power to make decisions affecting their classroom.

These examples demonstrate that all three schools were not successful in developing a districtwide common vision. Observations, interviews, and a review of district documents suggest individuals are unaware of, or have not internalized, their school mission. Definitions for innovations do not have common meaning between teachers and/or groups. The instability of a school's or administration's vision promotes the paradox: In each school, districtwide changes appeared blocked by internal or external forces. Therefore, it appeared teachers were safer promoting and protecting their own vision of a classroom than subscribing to a broader vision that places them at risk.

Dryden

Mission. The school lacks a common mission; as a result, individual teachers are confused about goals toward which they work, as part of a school. When teachers were asked about the school's mission, their comments included the following: "Educate children to be responsible people in life." "We talked about that at a meeting. Provide a safe, caring atmosphere for students to learn to their best capabilities." "A belief that all children can learn." A number of teachers responded, "We have one, but I don't know where it is right now." One teacher said, "[The superintendent/ principal] has a vision, but everyone needs to struggle in how to get there." When asked what the vision was, she did not know.

The administration used a slogan in an attempt to focus the district: "Failure-free by '93." The former principal reported that this put a sour taste in people's mouths. She said, "Teachers made sure no one failed. We found out that you cannot force someone to learn." The community thought the slogan meant only C's, B's, and A's would be given.

Definitions. Teachers had problems with programs introduced into the school, because no common definitions were established. Teachers and administrators could not agree among themselves how to define such common innovations as: outcome-based education (OBE), hands-on instruction, team teaching, cooperative learning, whole group and whole language instruction, and site-based management (SBM). Because they didn't understand the meaning or purpose of such innovations, teachers viewed them as restricting their ability to provide instruction. Some teachers claimed they could not teach certain math or reading concepts because the OBE curriculum would not allow it. One teacher reported many problems with the combination of all of these new programs. She said, "Science curriculum, they took away our textbooks, now we have to find our own materials. The math curriculum is not settled. We worked all the way through and they are not settled on the curriculum." She gave examples of gaps in the curriculum, and continued, "I see OBE limiting the teacher's ability to teach new thinking or expand when the kids are ready."

Elkin

Mission. The school district has published a formal plan to guide district operations. However, when teachers were asked about the strategic plan, mission statement, beliefs, goals, and action plans, they were unable to restate them in either specific or general terms. Teachers reported receiving copies of the plan, but could not locate them. Copies of the mission and belief statements were posted in the lounge and office, and printed in the teachers' and students' handbooks.

One teacher said, "The mission statement was watered down and can be interpreted several different ways." An administrator said, "The old mission statement dealt with the Hunter Model of Instruction [nationally known instructional format for classroom use, developed by Dr. Hunter, a professor of education]. We still use that, but we have broadened that approach." Neither individual could interpret the mission statement. Evidently, publishing information does not guarantee teachers can develop a common purpose for their actions.

Definitions. Teachers had no common understanding of new programs being introduced to the school. They reported varying definitions for whole language, whole group, hands-on instruction, OBE, or results-oriented curriculum (ROC), integrated curriculum, portfolios, and SBM. A teacher said, "I don't think there is a district definition of what whole language is. There are problems all right. Usually in in-services you get one person's view on how they perceive whole language." Another teacher said, "Part of the problem with whole language is it has not been defined. That model will not fit and the community would have a problem with that." SBM elicited similar comments. A teacher said, "They established a mission statement on SBM without training for the members who developed it [the mission statement]." Teachers reported various ideas about the definition of SBM: "SBM is people having a voice in what is going to affect them," "I would say, making decisions close to the people that the decision is going to affect," and "To me it is the ability of the teachers and principal to run things the way we want to."

Skyland

Mission. The school district published a formal strategic plan to guide the district's planning for improvement. The strategic plan included a mission statement, essential learning outcomes, and action plans designed to carry out the mission and support the essential learning outcomes. Teachers could not state either the mission statement or the essential learning outcomes. One teacher said, "I cannot repeat it. It has changed. The new one has more of an academic focus. The mission was to meet the needs of children in the classroom. So, we decided to go with research." The mission statement was posted on the wall of her room, and she faced it during this interview. Another teacher said, "You mean the mission statement?" She stood up and retrieved two laminated sheets from behind a cabinet. She told the researcher, "We were given posters of 'Essential Learning Outcomes' and the 'Mission Statement.' I don't know if it affected my area that much."

Teachers were concerned that the public did not understand the intent of the essential learning outcomes. The researcher asked a teacher, "How would you defend the changes?" She said, "That's a good question. I don't think there is a good defense. The essential learning outcomes... were to measure what the student values.... What do we want a person to look like at the end of their school journey?" She said that the wording of the essential learning outcomes caused the public to think that the school was not teaching reading, writing, and math. Another teacher said, "Basically, [the community] did not understand. They thought it was moving away from academics, because of talking about the student as friend, learner, citizen, producer.... The public still thinks we're moving away from the basics."

Definitions. Definitions vary for key words used by teachers and administrators to describe programs. Titles assigned to particular programs are not clear parts of the school system's vocabulary. For example, teachers used the terms "site-based management," "site-based decision-making," "site decision-making," and "group decision-making" interchangeably. When one teacher was asked, "What is SBM?" she responded, "That is the key question; people don't have a clear philosophy. It's kinda, sort of, maybe, in administration. It has a lot of gray areas about SBM. They do not know." Another teacher answered, "[SBM means] I have more say on what goes on in my job and school." A specialty teacher said, "The board still has the authority to set the mission. Every school needs to have flexibility to manage the school day to day, and the teachers make decisions for kids that work for them. As long as it is toward the common goals." An administrator asked about SBM said, "The method suggested by Kaizen [the management philosophy described in Imai, 1986]. The concept of continual improvement." In fact, these are two different programs.

Similar definition problems plagued other programs. Teachers used the term "action research" to describe an in-service activity. Teachers' definition of this term included: "This is an in-service where staff reads and studies the areas they want to study." "We wanted the staff to research new ways of doing things to improve. Examples are inclusion, hands-on, and research for better ways of doing things." A teacher who was promoting "action research" showed the researcher the book that guides her perception of this approach. The book clearly defines the relationship of six terms and a process to focus research, guiding the effort toward an evaluation. The book had apparently not been read either by the individual promoting "action research" or by others involved with the project.

The researcher probed definitions of terms the superintendent used during an interview. He stopped during the researcher's questioning and injected, "I never use buzz words.... We pick them [buzz words] for the new curricular areas that are not commonly defined by curricular areas [apparently meaning that they create terms for newly established instructional programs to avoid conflict with teachers and/or community members]."

GUIDELINES

Without clear visions of what a school is to accomplish, it is not surprising when schools lack clear guidelines to plan improvements. Administrators and teachers contribute to the paradox in their attempts to implement changes to improve the school. Without a clear vision or guide to direct improvement, any innovation may be promoted. Administrators or teachers attend a workshop or read about a program to improve student learning. The innovation is then brought into the district and urged or forced formally or informally on other teachers.

Each school has attempted several innovations over the past 5 years. Each was implemented on faith that the innovation would improve student learning. Each innovation was carried out without predetermining a measure to evaluate whether the innovation was effective. In no case did systematic follow-through ensure that the innovation was implemented as its authors intended, or, indeed, implemented at all. Naturally, teachers resisted change and tried to maintain the status quo. As one teacher said, "Why change? Next year there will be something else they want us to try."

Compounding the problem, no one in any of the schools determines whether the innovation duplicates existing programs or provides something new. All existing programs remain in place, and the innovation simply increases the teachers' work loads.

The lack of guidelines promotes the paradox. Administrators, teachers, and parents "preset the agenda" to promote or block change, maintaining or enhancing their own visions through this political technique. Of course, use of this technique requires power and influence, which sets an example that reinforces the idea that power and influence are important to protect the teachers' vision.

The rest of this section looks at these problems of: administration, teachers, follow-through, no dropping of overlapping programs, and preset outcomes.

Dryden

Administration. The administration developed written plans based on information gathered at a community strategic planning meeting. These included two documents, "Business/Marketing Plan" (administrative plan to sell the restructuring plan to the community) and "Expectations of the Board of Education for 1993–1994" (goals established by the board). The "Expectations" document outlines priorities to achieve quality teaching. When teachers were asked about the documents, they claimed not to know about them. However, when a principal from another school in the district and former principal of Dryden's school was asked about planning, she said, "We don't have a specific plan. It is troubleshooting and putting out brush fires, or following board directives on test results."

Later in the interview she commented on Dryden's superintendent/current principal's view of improvement. She said, "He has looked at problems as a system problem." This observation seemed confirmed in interviewing the superintendent/principal.

The current superintendent/principal was asked why he had taken the time to hold the strategic planning meeting and develop the planning documents. He said, "We started to move with the Fish Commission, President's Summit, Business Round Table, 20 Standards, and Scandia Report, all having the same agenda: to improve education for all kids. All were in response to 'A Nation At Risk.' We, the leadership team, talked about the purpose and the focus to improve student learning. In other words we talked at the board meetings. We talked about what was happening in the external environment and how that was going to affect our school."

The researcher found no evidence that the administration used data to predict the results of their strategy for improvements.

Teachers. Teachers view strategies for improvement in three ways: as mandates down from the administration, as upward strategies that bypass the administration, or as philosophical. They cited restructuring, OBE, and other programs brought in by the administration as top-down management that forced teachers to change. Two teachers reported bypassing the administration and going directly to the board to get improvements they needed. Two other teachers reported making changes without letting the administration know. When teachers were asked about formal procedures to introduce ideas for improvement, they claimed that none existed.

Follow-through. The researcher found only two administrative actions were taken that were mandated in the "Business/Marketing Plan": conducting a survey for parents, and plotting a few test scores. The administration did not present the teachers with results from either action or follow-up on other intended actions. Consequently, interest in the administration's plan decreased over time. Both the former principal and some teachers said interest in OBE was decreasing. Teachers reported that they had not tested students to verify learning, and had decreased the amount of retesting to provide more teaching time.

No Dropping of Programs. Teachers were asked, "Are programs ever dropped?" A teacher with 25 years in the school said, "No one ever says 'we're dropping this'; it dies on the vine." Other teachers agreed that programs are never dropped. One said, "Now we teach both [former method and new], not because we like them, but because we have to." She explained that she always teaches both her old material and the new, so she has good results. She said, "You know another program is going to come along next year, and no one ever tells you stop doing the last change."

Preset Outcomes. Administrators and teachers can employ two means of presetting (or predetermining) outcomes, to accomplish results they deem important. To predetermine the outcome of a meeting, administrators can name individuals to committees, or in other ways place them strategically where they can support the administration's position. The resulting votes control the meeting's results. After a meeting of this type, one teacher said, "Their mind was made up before the meeting.... It was a waste of time." Another said, "The decision was already made before the committees were formed." The school's informal leadership also employs this method, using the administration to place key people on committees to, for example, hire new teachers.

The second method used by both administrators and informal leaders is to claim that research is so convincing it should determine the direction the school must take. Both administrators and teachers send out materials or place them where others will read them. Teachers were observed using this to ensure that they could continue using new and/or different programs.

Elkin

Administration. The Elkin administration actively verbally promotes school improvement, but the data suggest that teachers do not receive or use formal guidelines to work toward common goals. They are confused by the administration's multiple statements. The district's strategic planning process produced a mission statement, belief statements, and 10 goals, each accompanied by an action plan to guide the district's activities. The administration published this plan and distributed it to the schools. Two teachers reported that the Director of Special Education provided them with regular progress reports. One teacher said, "They are checking to see if the steps of the plans are carried out and offer feedback on a regular basis." The other teacher said, "Our school has *five* goals that were typed up to work on. The director publishes a report each quarter on how we're doing on the goals." However, the number of goals was not accurate (there are 10), and how much of the plan had been implemented was not known. Generally, teachers were aware that the district had used a strategic planning process, but were not knowledgeable about the plan's contents or purpose.

A teacher indicated that the superintendent was not effective in setting a direction for the district. He said, "Physically he is a figurehead. Our superintendent uses the words 'cutting edge'; as a result, we don't know where the cutting edge is. He asks for so many things we have to turn him down. We don't have a hook to put our hat on."

Teachers. Teachers offered descriptions, different from those of the administration, of the process of planning for improvement. All teachers stated that they had volunteered or been signed up for committees. Teachers feel they have a say in district and school improvements, although the researcher found no evidence to support teachers' claims that they have clear guidelines to plan improvements on a district or school level.

One group of teachers views all change as top-down management. A teacher in this group said, "The decisions are made for us." Other teachers feel empowered. A teacher said, "We want people to feel empowered and have a voice. I am not sure it feels that way to the staff. The strategic plan is to find what is supported so it will be successful. The committees work toward a clear mission." Another teacher said, "SBM is creeping into the district. It is not going to be hard for the teachers. It is going to be hard for administration."

One teacher with more than 20 years in the school said, "I have very little to do with administration up on the hill. Among the staff members we call it the 'Ivory Tower' and they sit in the air-conditioning and we are down in the trenches.... This is OK, I can teach the way I want to."

Follow-through. Although the district has a strategic plan for improvement, plans for implementation meet varied success. The superintendent published a report that outlined in general terms the progress the district had made toward each of the 10 goals; however, 4 months after publication, the district had not taken action to further achieve the goals. Three months after school started, the building principal reported that goals for the school had not been established. When teachers were asked about their committee work, they reported meeting, but could not state what they had accomplished. A teacher with more than 20 years in the district said, "We do get bogged down in something. The committees work on things until they are able to solve the problem." He reported that one committee had not reported progress to the administration in 2 years.

No Dropping of Programs. Teachers reported introducing new programs and using old materials, but did not say they dropped programs or stopped using materials. A teacher said, "We're improving the use of computers...hands-on in science...whole language.... You don't have isolated skills. I try to balance the best of both. We don't know what skills they need when." When a teacher was asked directly, "How does the school drop old programs?" she said, "We need a way to do that."

Preset Agendas. Teachers perceive that anyone who wants to be on a committee has the opportunity; however, the data suggest that selected people were placed on the committees. A teacher explained: "The community is heavily involved in the strategic planning process.... Our director of special education formed a committee.... There was an advertisement in the paper. The main people were handpicked by the director of special education and the superintendent from the respondents." The researcher asked, "How were staff members selected?" She said, "We asked for volunteers. The administrative team picked people from each school." A board member verified this story when he was asked to respond to the following statement: "The administration placed key people on committees to achieve the outcome they wanted. The teachers not 'in the know' are upset about the favoritism." He said, "Absolutely, we stack the deck, no question about it." In fact, an administrator said he talked with Kathy El about the strategic planning process: "Yes, we talked about the committees and their context and how the committees are structured." The Elkin principal said, "You always question if you put the people that are against everything on committees."

Skyland

Administration. In the development of the strategic plan, postelection, the administration involved 350 people, including teachers, administrators, parents, and community members. They chose this development model because they had been told that a high level of involvement by people affected by the plan would promote its widespread acceptance. To help ensure the plan's success, the district published a detailed account of the mission statement, essential learning outcomes, and action plans. They created laminated posters outlining the plan. These were distributed to teachers and posted in teachers' lounges, administrative offices, and public areas in school district buildings.

The superintendent said, "The strategic plan builds the framework, and then the employees of the organization are allowed to fill in the center the way they need to within the framework. We reward people for imagination in this process." The researcher asked, "The framework, where does that come from?" The superintendent said, "Here we look at the work already done. We put together a leadership team to do just that. Now we have the parents, community, teachers, and administration on the team. They decided to revisit the strategic plan. That influenced several things: portfolios to measure individual learning, development of work teams, and other committees.... That is the power of it. When you move through change it alters the fabric of the school."

Other administrators and teachers are less optimistic about the stability of the strategic plan. An administrator said, "People are not linear or sequential or scientifically logical.... There are loops in that you don't anticipate [new conservative board members]. ... the high degree of threat that the change meant for people [conservatives and liberals].... People took the change personally and there was a lack of trust [between factions]. Now I am working on the backlash of personal trust and the change [trying to bring the sides together]. It [the backlash] is what we [supporters of the postelection strategic plan] felt from the conservative faction that won the school board election." A central office administrator said, "I would have never started this if I knew what was going to happen [pressure from the new conservative faction]."

Pressure from the new board members jeopardizes the strategic plan's strategy. One teacher said, "I think their agenda is to block any changes to the [postelection] mission statement until the next election.... They think they will control the board and be able to drop all the plans." The building principal confirmed that progress on reaching a compromise is slow.

Teachers. Teachers who want to retain the ability to implement changes in their classrooms want the current management system to remain in place. These teachers perceive they can currently do whatever they feel is best for kids. They support the administration's strategy, which is aligned with their perception of how a school should operate. They are working to maintain the current system of management derived from the postelection strategic plan, because they like the direction the school is going.

Teachers who do not support the innovations being carried out are working toward change that will reflect their perceptions of how a school should operate. They support the new board members by placing pressure on administration. They also give the conservatives information that supports returning the district to its old management procedures.

Again, Sam S1, unlike the other teachers, uses a strategy that reframes her program so it appeals to both the old and new board members.

Follow-through. The strategic plan designated specific committees to develop action plans that would direct activities in the district. A new board member said, "I watched the way the plan was implemented through action committees. The action committees were to develop activities to support the actions to be taken. Teams were not finished with their work. The teams were implementing things before they were finished or had reported their plan to the board for approval." The superintendent reported that the district had not done a good job of monitoring or recording the progress of every committee. He knew that some committees had not reported their work.

The principal's strategy is to implement an innovation and then respond to problems. She said, "I prefer having changes this way. It is better than sitting around and talking about it for 2 years." The researcher asked what kind of measures she used to evaluate the innovations. She said, "You can't know if the change takes unless you can follow the teacher around to see if it took." The data (or lack thereof) suggest that no one follows through to determine whether an innovation, once adopted, has been implemented, or whether it has resolved the problem for which it was introduced.

No Dropping of Programs. Teachers reported introducing new programs and using old materials, but did not indicate that they dropped programs or stopped using materials. A teacher with more than 20 years in the school said, "I don't believe in throwing things out. We still have basal readers and we use them. We support them with additional materials. We are fortunate to have the materials.... It is easier to use the basal readers. The basal is more interesting and richer. The use of the basal is combined with using the whole language approach to reading.... Why throw out what is working!" Another teacher said that students came to his room with widely different skills because teachers have never been told to stop using old programs when new ones are introduced: "People sat in their own little kingdoms. They could do what they wanted.... All the changes have confused teachers as to what is expected, accepted, and acceptable." Another teacher said, "We don't drop the old, we just add the new to it. We never really drop any program." The superintendent confirmed these teachers' comments: "We don't make announcements that we're dropping or adding."

Preset Agenda. Teacher, administrators, and community members debate whether the administration preset the agenda for developing and implementing the strategic plan. When an old board member was asked about this he said, "Lovely political statement; it is not true. There was a continuous effort not to stack the deck. We put out an all-call to whoever wanted to be involved." Two administrators and a teacher explained that the district had sent people to community groups and churches to ask people to be on the committees.

But the new board members had a different view of the process. In the newspaper they accused the administration of selecting committee members who followed their preset agenda to achieve the administration's desired outcome for the strategic plan. A new board member said, "Naturally teachers would focus on these issues. This is one of the problems. They want to do everything by committees that are over-staffed with teachers."

Members of the old board accused the new board members of having a preset agenda aligned with the religious right. The researcher could not find data to support this assertion. But the membership lists did show committees had a majority of school personnel on them. Whether this means teachers are willing to be good citizens, or are protecting their vision, is a matter of interpretation.

The teachers' informal leadership presets the agenda for staff meetings as described in the Leadership dimension, under Informal Leadership.

SUMMARY/COMMENT

The strategies used by leadership in the subject schools did not accomplish a balance. In fact, the plans used to develop a clear mission were thwarted by either the internal or external cultures. Hmaidan (1991) suggests that strategies accomplish the school's mission through regular interaction with the external and internal environments. This suggests that Purkey and Smith's (1985) idea that schools be mandated to adopt characteristics perceived as "effective" may in fact promote teachers to take action. Teacher may use their power and influence to protect their vision of a good classroom, before considering a global school improvement plan. The study also supports Lezotte's (1992a) claim that schools lack a method for dropping outdated programs. These findings suggest that alternative strategies be considered which may help balance the needs of the external and internal cultures (Blankstein, 1993; Bonstingl, 1993; Brandt, 1993a,b; Deming, 1993; Holt, 1993; Macchia, 1993; Rankin, 1992; Rhodes, 1992; Juran, 1992; Glasser, 1990a).

CHAPTER 10

The Structure

INTRODUCTION

So far, we have been considering four dimensions that affect all organizational systems, including school systems: the culture of the external environment, the culture of the internal environment, leadership, and strategy. In this chapter, we will consider the structure, the way these four dimensions fit together in the system to produce results. The structure determines how informal and formal interactions among people in the external and internal school environments influence instructional coordination, provision of services, methods of improvement, and administrative functions, including allocation of assets. In other words, the structure controls how schools conduct their business. The end results of that business—either real, measurable results or perceived results—can either enhance or threaten the cultural and individual visions of good schools and classrooms.

When visions conflict with each other, leadership will try to balance them by carrying out a strategy to change the organizational structure. You can see that a system feeds back on itself; each of the various dimensions of the system has consequences that affect all other dimensions.

Our schools have strangleholds around them. This is the result of formal and informal leadership groups attempting to carry out strategies that will enhance or maintain their ideal vision of school (recall Fig. 4.2). The external and internal environment culture's leadership compete to control the decision-making process using power and influence to protect what they value, their vision. In the three schools studied, formal and informal processes are allowed to mandate change controlled by either formal or informal leadership. Each school's structure allowed competing factions to block their school's improvement efforts in a constant struggle to achieve one vision, then another.

If we are to release the stranglehold on our schools, we must change the structure; otherwise, we will continue to provide results that cause the public to attack schools for producing outcomes that do not match their ideal visions.

We can consider the structural dimension both as something unique and isolated from the other dimensions, and as a combination of all of the other dimensions. Thinking about the system as a whole will help you understand the importance of finding the key patterns in the systemic structure. Such patterns are known, unknown, and unknowable; they are visible and invisible. These key patterns create the most significant barriers to school improvement. If a school organization wants to produce different results, it must change the key patterns within the overall structure.

Remember that the total organizational structure has produced the problems that will be described in this chapter. *Do not blame the people involved!* They are doing exactly what they have been trained to do: to protect their visions of good schools and classrooms.

The system contains external and internal cultures. Each proposes changes that will result in changes in structure. The system also contains formal and informal leadership that contain groups and individuals that may cause or block change. In this chapter, we will look at the organizational structure in the following categories: small groups and individual influence, methods for improvement, instructional coordination, administration, conflicting needs, and other school services. For each, we will revisit the three school systems.

STRUCTURE DIMENSION

Small Groups and Individual Influence

The structure permits small groups and individuals to influence school activities. The findings in the external environment culture dimension explained how parents and community members use power to control the school (Chapters 5 and 6); the internal environment culture dimension explains the use of power by teachers to promote or maintain their visions of a classroom (Chapter 7). These individuals and groups interact with the formal and informal leadership, who control the strategy to promote or block change. When small groups or individuals cause change, the structure may change, producing a different system than before. Alternatively, groups or individuals may block change. This leaves the structure as it has been, and the results of the structure remain unchanged.

This analysis suggests that the system itself can prevent schools from producing results that the external and internal environment culture will accept. The system teaches people that they need power and influence to protect what they value, thus creating and promoting the paradox, namely, teachers need power and influence in order to work toward improving student learning.

The communities studied varied in how their formal and informal leadership structure used power and influence to conduct their business. However, their activities appeared to have similar outcomes, continuous cycles of change and instability. Specific groups in each community are described under the headings of Parents, Teachers, and Administration.

Dryden

Parents. Parents caused changes by contacting the board, administrators, and/or individual teachers with requests to affect the classroom. Board members report that, at community functions, parents tell them they've asked administrators to consider making specific changes. When parents come to board meetings, the Dryden board resists passing resolutions for change. The researcher questioned two board members about a case in which a parent forced a change in a special education program. At first, the board members did not recall the case, but after they heard more about it, they claimed it had been turned over to the administration, which was told to extend the program. One board member said, "She volunteered.... I have a tendency to listen more to the people that constantly talk to me and are involved with the school." This case created concern among teachers, who talked about the parent in the lounge. They were concerned that the parent would control their classrooms.

Teachers. Lori D1, who has been in the district for less than 15 years, said, "[The superintendent/principal] realizes the teachers can be an enemy for him," indicating this teacher controls the decision-making process by controlling the administration. She and other teachers she influences talk to the administrator and set the agenda for the school. A teacher with 25 years in the district recognizes and resents the newer group's influence. (Years of service in the school seemed to have status before restructuring.) This elder teacher avoids the administration and talks directly to members of the board of education about her concerns. She "does what she feels is best for kids in her classroom." The superintendent/principal was never observed asking her to change or do anything outside the normal schedule of activities.

Administration. The administrative team has influenced the board of education in the past, but has lost some power as a result of pressure on the board from teachers, parents, and community members. The superintendent/principal and administrative team influenced the board to restructure the school and to provide money for new programs. But since the restructuring, the board has pressured the administration into reducing teacher complaints to the board. As a result, the administration has lost influence with the board.

Elkin

Parents. Teachers reported that individual parents and groups of parents can cause a teacher or the administration to change what is happening in the school. Teachers say that "just one parent" has the power to disrupt their normal teaching schedules. A teacher told the researcher that a parent demanded a progress report on her child every week. When the researcher asked another teacher about the weekly reports, she said, "We had one that wanted them every day." Another teacher reported a parent who objected to a science project. She said, "This parent wanted a committee to write up how animals will be treated in the classroom." Two teachers mentioned a parent who believed her child was being treated badly by other children. One of the teachers said, "The whole school had to write up their guidance program to prove to the parents all children were taught how to react to [the student]."

A teacher commented, "The PTO, they have impacted [teaching], some leaders are strong-willed and want their way." She told a story about an occasion on which the PTO president controlled the principal: "The chair of the PTO said to [the principal], 'Don't ask [the teacher] what she wants, tell her what to do.'" The affected teacher confirmed that the principal then made the requested change without asking her opinion.

Administrators and teachers report that small groups of parents affect both the school and the school district. The principal told a story about a parent who had a conflict with a science teacher. A teacher verified the story: "[The teacher] wanted a hands-on program [the parent wanted a traditional program].... To compromise [to meet the parent's expectations], the district bought a textbook [which the teacher used to teach hands-on]." Both the teacher and the principal believe this previous experience with textbooks over whole language instruction influenced the purchase of textbooks for the science program. The superintendent told a different story about a group of men from the country club, led by a parent, who forced the introduction of a particular program. After the parent's child completed the program, it was dropped.

Teachers. The principal said, "I do not feel teachers should have the freedom to use only trade books, or a total hands-on curriculum in science and math. I am concerned that the teachers will vary so much that children will have a difficult time moving between grade levels and schools. If teachers have too much freedom to teach what they want, the next teachers will have two sets of students with different instructional backgrounds." But the principal's expressed beliefs differed from his actions. When teachers asked the principal about classroom schedules, activities, and use of materials, he gave them options. Furthermore, observation suggested that teachers, rather than the principal, set the school's agenda.

The district has a history of teachers setting agendas. The superintendent said, "[This school district] is known historically as a district with a great deal of teacher autonomy.... What has happened...due to some of the autonomy some subjects were not being taught. So we started saying, 'Starting with a blank schedule, show us where you teach what.'" Half of the teachers, according to the principal, turned in the schedules that matched those requested by the administration.

Administration. One board member said she contacted the principals for input before board meetings, but reported that she votes her own mind. The data suggest that the administration achieves power and/or status through others, whose ideas administrators promote. For example, the administration initiated the strategic planning process; but when two teachers perceived the plan for their building as a battleground between the old and the new guard, the teachers blocked the plan in the school.

Skyland

Parents. Individual parents have caused teachers to modify the instructional program in their classrooms. Teachers who reported that parents contacted them, also reported that they responded. One teacher said, "I did not change that much [classroom activities].... This year I plan to change a lot [make changes that match the conservative group's agenda]. I am planning to tell parents more of what they want to hear." Another teacher reported putting on a play for parents to demonstrate what the students had learned. A nontenured teacher said, "I have modified my program. I would like to do it differently." A teacher with more than 15 years in the district said, "To me [parents] are allies, but I'm doing things to make sure they are. I have never had to deal with a difficult parent, because I take precautionary measures to avoid that." An old board member said that the relationship between parents and teachers has changed: "It's become adversarial rather than cooperative."

Teachers. Teachers individually and collectively cause the administration to take action. Three teachers insist that discipline at the school is out of control and the principal is responsible. The principal spends time solving discipline problems and establishing ways to measure improvements. She uses data she has gathered to demonstrate to the entire staff that discipline problems are decreasing. Her attention to discipline keeps her out of the classrooms and reduces her involvement in planning activities. Observation suggest teachers generally did not want any administrator in their classrooms.

Administration. During the strategic planning process, preelection, administrators influenced each other and the board of education. An old board member reported that the former superintendent had helped the board focus its efforts. He said, "The board set the areas to work on...this process worked well...now with the election all of this could change.... I feel sorry for the staff. Part of this is the great mistrust of teachers by the new board members. The resistance comes from a mental model that says, 'It wasn't done that way when we went to school. So prove to me it is better."

Methods for Improvement

Methods for improving the schools (committees, meetings, and training) are subject to all of the variables listed in the strategic dimension. All of these methods are also subject to the use of power and influence by individuals and small groups.

In Dryden, teachers described a committee on which all members worked cooperatively. Teachers on the committee reported that the results exceeded their expectations. But teachers who were members of another committee reported being controlled. One teacher said, "It turned out whoever had the most people at the meeting won out."

In Elkin, teachers were divided in their perceptions of committee work. Some teachers described a cooperative effort, while others on the same committee reported that specific teachers controlled the committee with disappointing results.

In Skyland, teachers reported and observation verified that the committee work was unfocused, wasted time, and produced results that were open to many different interpretations. Nonetheless, teachers defended the use of committees.

These examples suggest several conclusions. First, committees may be more productive when all members perceive them as cooperative ventures. Second, committees that are controlled by a few people produce results that other members have difficulty accepting. Finally, committees that function cooperatively but cannot reach consensus change nothing. These conclusions indicate that control issues contribute to the existing paradox, the need for influence to create change. Teachers on a cooperative committee accomplished more than they were asked to do. Committees controlled by a few produced results other teachers resented. When committees were absent of formal or informal leadership's control, members were happy, but no real change occurred.

Observations of meetings held in each school verified that the informal leadership controlled the outcomes of the meetings by using specific strategies to promote or block improvements.

Training teachers to carry out innovation also reflected problems that fall within the structure dimension. Such problems are specifically lack of clear purpose, lack of follow-through, and lack of evaluation methods for innovation. Lack of training and reinforcement necessary to complete the implementation of changes compounded these problems. Teachers reported insufficient training and offered multiple definitions and descriptions of specific innovations and their intended purposes. Presented with unclear purposes, teachers developed their own definitions of innovations and their own ideas of how to implement them. In each school, teachers reported similar problems: being overwhelmed by changes, abandoning innovations before they were implemented, and having too much to learn in too little time. Teachers resorted back to their own vision, to cope during times of rapid changes.

Dryden

Committees. Teachers want to be involved with committees that affect their school and/or classroom, but they have different views of committee work, depending on their perceptions of its function, time lines, expectations, boundaries, and impact. When teachers perceive committee work as a cooperative effort with reasonable time lines; when they see results that meet or exceed their expectations, and that also clearly help improve student learning in the classroom, then they report feelings of accomplishment and reward. The members look forward to carrying out the committee's ideas for improvement. However, when teachers perceive committee work as controlled by a minority, with outcomes dictated to meet other people's expectations; when they forecast results that negatively affect their classrooms, then teachers resist carrying out the committee's work. Committee members report frustration at attempts to negate the committee's conclusions or to change the boundaries.

A team of teachers who worked to improve the math curriculum at their grade level demonstrated positive feelings toward committee work. They reported cooperating, having time to work, exceeding their expectations, and working within the boundaries set by the administration. They were proud of their work and looked forward to carrying out their ideas.

Teachers reported the work of other committees as frustrating. The district was a member of a consortium, several area school districts pooling resources, to develop OBE curriculum. A teacher who participated in consortium meetings said, "Some of the teachers felt they did not need this…. It turned out whoever had the most people at the meeting won out in setting the objective. [A particular school district] was the dominating school. Our district didn't have much pull. During the process they tried to get rid of textbooks. I am pleased with the math and science texts we have."

Other teachers also reported problems with committees. A teacher was frustrated with her assignment: "I was never trained on writing objectives." Another teacher said, "The school dealt with the concepts but did not get at the root cause of the problem. We spend a lot of time sharing ideas, but they don't get placed into practice." Reports of other teachers and a review of relevant documents verified these comments.

Meetings. Staff meetings were used to bring staff members together, give and receive information, and make decisions. The Dryden meetings were held inconsistently, agendas were not followed, and minutes were not consistently kept or published. Regular staff meetings were scheduled every other Friday, starting at 8:10 AM, but they usually began 10 to 20 minutes late with only half of the staff present. As the meetings progressed, staff continued to arrive and leave. Administrators regularly canceled meetings minutes before they were scheduled to start, and announced unscheduled meetings without warning, before or after school.

Meeting agendas were usually placed on a blackboard by the superintendent/principal in the meeting area; however, once a meeting began, the agenda was meaningless. A group of teachers would reframe agenda items to discuss or avoid discussion of specific issues. This practice was observed most often when the agenda included parents' requests and building improvements.

Because meeting minutes were not regularly recorded or published, a few individuals controlled the consequences of any meetings. Formal meeting minutes were sometimes typed, but not always distributed. Teachers who could not directly influence the administration kept personal minutes.

Teachers responded differently to these irregularities. Teachers who set the agenda had no complaints about when and how meetings were conducted. Other teachers were ambivalent or upset that they had no control over the decision-making process.

Observations of Dryden district meetings revealed similar problems with time, agendas, and minutes.

Training. The district's training program does not support changes in technology and new programs. The administration provides computers and software to make the teachers' tasks easier, but teachers received no follow-up support to help them use the technology. A special education teacher was provided a computer to write reports on. Two years after she received the computer, she did not know that more than one file is saved on a disk, what a template is, or how to edit old documents without retyping the document. Observation revealed that other teachers and support staff also lack computer skills.

Administrators used districtwide in-services and other meetings outside school to introduce new programs, but teachers report there is no follow-through. OBE, for example, was introduced at a districtwide in-service. A teacher said, "Administration had hired this [individual] to come into the district and tell us about OBE." Some teachers were given additional training, and they were to train the others. However, they were not given time to do this training. Another teacher verified this story, adding, "We do something and don't follow up."

The administration drops programs by not following through. A teacher said, "I thought site-based management would go over. A group of teachers went for training.... [The superintendent/principal] appointed the local business manager to head the effort. We've never had a meeting since.... It's just been shot down."

The following story illustrates the consequences of training lapses in the district: After a playground accident, a child could not move. A teacher panicked and ran through the halls to the office. The secretary attempted to contact two people who had been trained to handle health emergencies, but the communications equipment was broken. During this time, an aide picked the child up. The teacher ran back to the playground, and by chance, one of the people designated to handle emergencies saw her and went out to the playground. The child went to the doctor with a parent and fortunately was fine.

The researcher found that an in-service session had been provided for emergency training, and a written plan outlined procedures. However, the procedures had never been practiced and the communications equipment had not been repaired despite five work orders. This example demonstrates that the Dryden district does not follow up to ensure that equipment is used. Training is ineffective, and appropriate procedures are not tested or implemented.

Consistency. Dryden teachers agree that methods for improvement are introduced too rapidly to allow them to keep up. A teacher said, "Day to day we all try to focus on kids and what has to be taught and learned. Everything seems to be so overwhelming, there is so much change." Other teachers also felt overwhelmed. "There have been so many changes," one said. "People are just doing the best they can in the situation. There is not a good set of rules. There is a lot of variability." Another teacher said, "It is change all the time. Teachers try to survive with the job." One teacher indicated the consequences of overwhelming, rapid change: "Teachers are willing to go through change, but the self-preservation issue comes in when the changes don't go as far as they thought it would. Then the next change doesn't get the effort it needs."

Elkin

Committees. Teachers generally support the committee structure for making improvements, but individual Elkin teachers view committee work differently, based on their perceptions of overlap in assignments, time requirements, expectations, boundaries, and impact. One teacher said, "The school has many committees that take a lot of time. I have eight regular committee meetings a month and four additional for M-teams [a group of professional staff that recommends services for special needs students.] and parents. The committees take time away from students and doing a better job, but I do not see any other way to have input from everyone without a committee structure."

Another teacher said the process of making changes varies: "It all depends on the change. Different rationale for different changes. If it is a school policy or discipline, the school uses committees." She described how the committees function by saying, "The committees will discuss the problem, look for solutions, talk about the effect of the solutions, and make suggestion to the staff or administration. This is a good process."

But other teachers did not agree that all committees function well, and did not support the extensive use of committees. A teacher on the district reading committee called it "the committee from hell." One teacher commented on relationships within a particular committee: "It did not work well, because people would not reach consensus.... People get their minds fixed on what is [not what could be]." Another teacher said, "The committees are overdone.... We need to reduce the number of committees and coordinate what they are doing." A teacher reported being on what she called the "decision-making committee." She said, "The committee established a subcommittee that was assigned the same task as a standing committee [a permanent committee previously established]. One was not necessary." Another teacher complained, "The administration does not set the boundaries for the committee work. The administration creates an illusion that the teachers have control and [we] really don't. Teachers would rather have the boundaries." Although one teacher insisted, "Committees keep working until they solve the problem," another disagreed: "There is no follow-through. There are a lot of plans made and not carried out. You start plans and they don't get carried out before new ones are started."

Administrators confirmed these concerns. An administrator said, "I am aware of overlaps..., but I get resistance from teachers. They complain about having to be on so many committees, but they complain when they do not have a voice. It is evident that the people don't want anything top-down, and want to participate, but are critical of the means." The superintendent said, "Teachers do not do a good job at distinguishing between district, ad hoc, building, and union committees.... Teachers feel if they're on a committee they have...power to act." At an informational meeting, the teachers' discussion illustrated the superintendent's observation. The teachers did not like a particular committee's recommendation, and they spent the meeting developing possible strategies to change the direction the committee was taking.

Meetings. The Elkin principal schedules, well in advance, three staff meetings each month. He publishes an agenda the day before each meeting. These meetings are designed to plan and coordinate school activities, and to share information. When asked how she feels about the school meetings, a teacher said, "It depends on which one, some go well, others, people are not organized and waste my time." Another teacher said, "Sometimes it is just a gripe session."

Meetings started a minimum of 10 minutes late, and people continued to arrive after the meetings began. The principal would begin with the published agenda. After discussing the first item, the teachers set the remainder of the agenda. A teacher commented, "The majority rules and everyone is not going off on their own tangent." Observation suggested that if Kathy E1, Ruth E2, Marge E3, or Mary E4 supported a resolution, it passed. Staff members directly influenced by these teachers led or blocked discussion until passage of the resolution was ensured. Teachers record the minutes of the meeting. Minutes from two meetings were never distributed. After each meeting, influential teachers talked with the principal, reinforcing decisions made at the meeting.

Training. Teachers say that the administration encourages them to learn about new programs, and provides in-services and workshop opportunities for teachers to be trained in new methods. Teachers who attend training sessions are positive about the knowledge they acquire, but both these teachers and others report that only a few teachers are trained in each new innovation. As a result, untrained teachers develop their own definitions of the innovation and their own ideas about how to implement it. A teacher said, "I knew we wanted a program for hands-on. Several people were trained in hands-on in science and math, but not all the teachers." Another teacher said, "The school provides training for some and expects the results to be integrated into the classroom." A teacher who discussed the school's difficulty with coordinating training said, "That's the problem with all programs, we don't get enough training to understand and use it. The same teachers always get to go and they are teaching us and don't have the time to do it."

Some teachers who did attend training could not relate it to their classroom or were unable to verbalize what they had learned. A teacher who reported that she had attended an in-service on inclusion with the Director of Special Education said, "The presenter was from California.... I could not do what she was asking. It was not within the law in Wisconsin, according to the director." Another teacher claimed to have had training on Deming's management theory. When the researcher asked what interested her about Deming, she could not state any of his concepts. Teachers perceive that they are being trained, but agree that there is no follow-through either in the school or the district.

Consistency. Teachers note that the school is trying to implement several innovations at one time. The rapid change causes stress on teachers who must attempt to make several changes at once. Because there is poor follow-through, some changes are abandoned before teachers learn them. A teacher said, "We are looking at a variety of things." She gave examples: cognitively guided math instruction, hands-on, and an integrated curriculum combining reading, science, and measurements. Another teacher complained, "Our district tries to focus on all the innovations at once, rather than learning one well, then taking another one. This wears us thin." A teacher reported the stressful effect of the innovations: "Research is coming out so quickly and it is always evolving in all academic areas. These are all different stressors. It is difficult to focus on student learning." Another teacher commented on the rapid changes: "When educational trends like OBE are thought of, you start informing yourself on that and before you get it started it's abandoned for a new fad."

Skyland

Committees. Teachers claim that the school uses committees to plan for improvements, but differ in their perceptions of the committees' functions and purposes. Comments by teachers suggest that committees are not focused and lack boundaries; that committee results are determined by chance; and that the committees' impact is not clear. One teacher said, "We have gone through so much change the last couple of years, both the committees and what they do. We just got into shared decision-making. Most of the time it's positive. Sometimes we would just like to be told and move on with it. I am not sure if there are written guidelines for the committees." Another teacher questioned about the work of a particular committee said, "I don't know which group discusses that. I am trying to think how the process works." She did not attempt to describe the process. The researcher questioned a teacher about the committees' goals. The teacher said, "They discuss specific goals and come up with a plan to get them into long term." The researcher asked, "What are the goals set by the group?" She answered, "They're not called that, committees then get together to work on one topic." A teacher who was asked, "Are there guidelines for the groups?" responded, "Yes, basically each group sets their own guidelines. They can address anything that has to do with your site." A teacher who was asked, "How are decisions reached?" said, "We try to reach a consensus." The researcher asked another teacher, "How many committees are you on?" She said, "[Of] school committees, citizenship and technology. Two, I am not on any others." The researcher probed, "How often do the committees meet?" She said, "Three or four times a year. [The principal] has them all set up."

Observation of a formal meeting of a grade-level team verified the committee's lack of focus. During a break from the meeting, the team gathered in the lounge. One teacher said to another, "I am tired of them getting their own way." Thirty seconds after this comment, two more teachers entered the lounge. One said, "We're writing up the direction for the...program." This conversation ended when the last teacher to enter the lounge said, "We need to write that down and make sure they do it."

The school formed a committee to change the report card format. When the committee reported on its recommendations, the researcher made the following observations: Vickie S7, S11, and S12 were upset with the new report card. S12 talked to Sam S1, who claimed that the teachers had not agreed on the topics listed on the new report card. S11 said, "We did not agree with this card as it is," pointing to two items: "understanding of community" and "Wisconsin lumbering." S12 said, "If I would have been there, this would not be on here." The report card was not changed.

Meetings. The Skyland principal schedules staff meetings twice a month. A teacher said, "[The principal] is a good organizer. When [she] runs a meeting, she stamps out a very productive meeting. She establishes an agenda that has times set for each item and the group usually sticks to it." Another teacher said, "Everyone is invited. That is important. This has not always happened. These meetings are directly tied to the team concept. No one feels that there is a power or control group.... Having all the staff members at the meetings prevents misinterpretation of information. It sets up a good communication system."

The researcher observed a meeting that started 10 minutes late. The principal had an agenda posted on a flip chart. As teachers arrived, individuals asked that additional items be placed on the agenda. Before the meeting started, the principal asked the teachers, "Is this agenda OK?" She accepted the nodding of heads and undistinguishable voices and noises as confirmation; the agenda was set. Jean S4, S8, and S9 addressed action items on the agenda. Sam S1, Renee S2, and Jean S4 addressed information items. S10 objected to a decision S8 was promoting. She was permitted to talk, but no one followed up on her suggestions. After this meeting, the principal asked the researcher, "Can't you feel the energy of the teachers working together?" Observation notes recording the meeting do not support her contention that teachers were working well together.

Training. Teachers say that the administration encourages them to attend in-services, but report that this has minimal impact on instruction. One teacher said, "We are given options of which in-services to attend. A sheet with several in-services is handed out to the teachers. The teachers are to check the ones they are interested in." The researcher observed such documents, given to teachers and placed in the lounge.

One teacher's comment about the impact of the in-service workshops is representative: "Any time spent in staff development is never enough time to tackle the project. It is so packed you feel incompetent and overwhelmed." She explained that the in-services and workshops try to cover so much ground that teachers do not have time to understand what is being taught. "The time available is so short that all you get is words. There is no time to practice what was to be learned or plan how this will fit into your classroom." She feels overworked during the in-services. She added, "We need to know what the innovations are, but there are so many you cannot learn how to use them in your classroom."

Another teacher said, "If a group of teachers want to explore an innovation they are supported. When they want it implemented...we only hear what they have learned and don't know if we are doing it correctly or not, because we were not trained. This adds variation between classrooms and grade levels."

Administrators were questioned about in-services and workshops, to check the teachers' claims. The superintendent said, "The district has been flooded with innovation. We are trying to narrow the focus. I could not get my arms around it. The discussion was focused on what we were not doing." He said the following innovations are being implemented: the portfolio system of grading, parent–teacher planning, individualized learning plans, integrated learning, literacy, "numeracy," and others. The superintendent was asked, "What is 'action research?'" in an attempt to verify the purpose of this training. He said, "We chose those words because they are not connected with curricular terms.... I don't know what the outcome is going to be. Maybe develop the question that needs to be researched, like site-based councils.... We are assuming we are making a situation where learning will become better."

An old board member was questioned about the district's in-service program. He said, "We have tried to focus our in-services around a theme. I have tried to get away from 'set and get' in-services. This is what we are all talking about. We need to leverage it to moving everyone in the same direction. We have been focused for 2 years. Now that is being challenged." The researcher found no evidence that the district had a theme for in-services, before or after the election.

Consistency. Teachers agree that the school is trying to carry out several innovations at one time, and that the rate at which innovations are introduced causes teachers stress. One teacher said, "There is a lot of change in this district. It moves quickly forward, sometimes too fast. You get overwhelmed with the expectation. So you cannot focus on the kids." Teachers cited the following innovations: hands-on learning, whole group, whole language, using trade books, curriculum compacting, OBE, cognitively guided instruction, numeracy math, portfolio assessment, literacy-based spelling, action research, and SBM. They felt they lacked sufficient time to learn and understand all of these changes. A teacher who says that the administration supports change complained, "They asked you to do stuff, but were not supportive of time. Now they did give us that. [The school district] is on the cutting edge. That is a problem sometimes. They were asking a lot to completely change our grading system. There was not time to adjust." She said that in one year, teachers had to change the grading system, and adjust their methods of teaching to fit the new system. "I went to every meeting and was totally frustrated, confused, and not supported.... On top of this there was not equitable time with the high school and middle school. They did not have to do portfolios. If this is such a great thing, why are we the only ones doing it?"

The researcher asked an administrator to respond to the teachers' complaints about rapid change and too little time to learn and apply the innovations. She said, "There is pain in a paradigm shift. All changes are based on gut feelings. If people do not feel it is better for them, they will not shift their paradigm. That is what we are fighting here. The community wants good schools, but [teachers say] the schools must function in the same manner as they are used to. When we changed the way we were doing things, to improve, there were parts of the community that did not want it to change. Some of the staff is the same way. That is why we are in the mess we are in. Change is always messy."

Instructional Coordination

Holding on to the old procedures has a negative effect on activities carried out during the school year. Kindergarten screening in Dryden offers a good example. The state does not mandate kindergarten screening; the information gathered during the screening duplicates information on file at the school; and teachers at other grade levels view it as a disruption. Two kindergarten teachers want children to be screened, the other two do not. Comments by teachers, administration, and support staff suggest that the screening functions primarily as a competition among the kindergarten teachers to gain parents' support and build status. Both teachers who want the screening have power and influence with teachers, administration, parents, and the community. In this way, they get the "best kids" for their classroom, according to a kindergarten teacher who opposes the screening. The screening provides a method for two teachers to maintain and build their status.

In Elkin, a reading teacher explained her frustration with the system of selecting students for her program. The formal rules changed each year, depending on state and federal mandates. Also, politics within the community and the school district changed local informal rules. The reading teacher had minimal influence in the school; therefore, according to the principal, she worried too much about not offending anyone. But two other teachers commented on which students should be in or out of her reading program. Observation suggested that she was right to worry, because other teachers did sanction her by making negative comments about her and her program.

Skyland made new plans for regularly scheduled activities each year, so that everyone had a chance to make changes. However, observation suggested that an influential group manipulated the decision-making so as not to offend anyone, while retaining programs unchanged.

Each of these examples demonstrates how the coordination of yearly activities meets a need of the organizational culture for ensuring status, self-preservation, or maintenance of the power structure. Yearly activities are used to protect what an individual or group values.

Teachers' work schedules and classroom activities affect teachers in a similar manner, and are similarly manipulated to promote the visions of individuals or small groups. Even though work schedules and the rules to support them are written, teachers do not always follow them. This establishes a system of favoritism, which builds status. If the schedule or rules threaten the status of a particular teacher or group, the schedule and rules are reframed or their effects are minimized. Each instructional coordination issue becomes a tool that the informal structure can use to build status or sanction others. These tools promote the social structure and protect its vision.

Dryden

Teachers differ in their perceptions of regularly scheduled yearly activities such as kindergarten screening. The kindergarten teachers want the screening to make a good impression on parents. They spend long hours decorating their rooms and use special planning time to prepare; despite this, the event revealed poor organization. On the day of the screening, both teachers and administrators had trouble finding needed materials. In frustration, a kindergarten teacher said, "Why are we doing this?" Another asked, "Why should we give up 2 days of teaching this year's students for next year's students when we cannot make suggestions to the parents?" A second-grade teacher said, "We don't need to do kindergarten screening. It is taking time away from my library time." The nurses told the researcher, "We really don't need to have it. Even the DPI [Department of Public Instruction] says we don't need to do it. We should drop it." And the former principal verified that all kindergarten testing occurred before the screening day. She said, "We do it because it has always been done in the district."

The yearly carnival, school pictures, and year-end activities—all of which required teachers' time to discuss what should be done and how they should be scheduled—also seemed to be done because they "always have been."

Teachers do not like guests or activities that change their daily schedules and affect their classrooms. A special education teacher said, "It takes away the sequence of activities to teach, who is to be doing what. All special education works well together. There is no communications to find out if everyone is getting to the student and we didn't miss anything." The researcher asked, "Why are you concerned about missing something?" She said, "It makes me feel like I am not doing my job." Other special education teachers report having big gaps in their schedules, which means they have several students at one time, and no students at other times. They would like a steady flow, and a constant number of students so they can work more with them. The researcher observed that some special education teachers had only one or two students in the morning and then several students in the afternoon without breaks between sessions.

Regular classroom teachers are upset with daily schedule changes that cause them to miss sending their kids to the specialty teachers (physical education, music, or art), or to miss scheduled preparation time. Teachers protect any time available for preparation, reporting that they have insufficient time during the day to prepare for students. They were vocal at meetings in opposition to rescheduling their time to accommodate special school activities and when they were asked to sacrifice prep time for special duties.

A general lack of agreement between written procedures and administrative practices required Dryden teachers to spend unnecessary time planning and coordinating recurring activities. Teachers spent time in the halls or in meetings talking about report cards, attendance, school rules, class trips, purchasing supplies, using grant money, and spelling bee contests. Each of these issues had been addressed in written documents the teachers received from the office, but teachers do not look at written procedures. Observation in the office made it clear why: The office does not follow the procedures either.

Report cards have a set schedule, but the administration changed the time line. A teacher said, "We thought we would have time to do them over break, but I guess not."

Elkin

Teachers reported concerns about the coordination of yearly activities, which required additional planning time. A teacher said these events are planned at meetings. "We usually discuss the events coming up and the building problems. It seems we need to find some way to put special events on a cycle. We have reading incentive programs, PTO, fun night, picnics, and open houses. Some of them take place during the day, others are after school, but it involves preparing the children for them. That takes time from the class time with students and away from preparation time."

A reading teacher complained, "This is the worst year ever. Every year is bad to get started." She told of struggling for a month every year to determine criteria for selecting participants in a reading program and developing a schedule. When asked, "Who sets the criteria?" she said, "I set the criteria up for the selection of students."

Observation data suggest that yearly events are not coordinated and teachers develop their own guidelines for activities. On days when special activities are scheduled, the principal and teachers ask each other what's going to happen and where the materials are. Minutes from staff meetings suggest recurring discussions and unscheduled annual tasks.

Elkin teachers do not like changes in daily work schedules that affect their classrooms. Special education teachers, specialty teachers, and regular education teachers struggle over the scheduling of special education students and special classes. A regular education teacher said, "You get a schedule for the specials [physical education, art, and music], which limits your ability to work with the kids."

The principal said that teachers ask him to schedule academics in the morning. A special education teacher complained, "The school always schedules reading the first thing in the morning. This causes my students to report to my room all at once. This causes an uneven work load. I could be more effective if I had a stable student load during the day."

Teachers protect preparation time before and during the school day. A teacher said, "We need time to work alone." Teachers do not have extra duties before school. The principal explained that he made a deal with the teachers. He would do outside duty in the morning to give teachers more prep time, if teachers would stay out of the lounge at that time. In fact, all but three teachers were in their rooms before school.

Teachers also negotiated early release days for planning. A teacher said, "That was a significant improvement, because it gave us additional planning time."

Teachers are upset when special activities overlap with preparation time. While teachers were talking about school-day activities planned to reward good behavior, a teacher said, "That is cutting into the time my kids are scheduled for PE." Her tone of voice indicated her displeasure.

Poor coordination of recurring activities and teachers' ignorance of written procedures wasted planning time. The teacher's handbook outlined procedures for scheduling minutes of instruction, preparing report cards, taking attendance, planning field trips, and purchasing supplies. The handbook also includes school rules, district goals, and other pertinent information. Teachers called this handbook the "red book" and a copy was kept in each classroom. During the study, not one book was moved from its storage place. However, teachers were observed asking the principal or the office secretary questions about subjects covered by the "red book." The principal's responses closely followed "red book" procedures.

Skyland

Teachers use planning time to coordinate yearly activities. Two groups of teachers were observed as they planned and carried out an annual activity. Each group was given one full day for planning, while substitute teachers taught their classes. An early release day provided an additional half-day for planning. Both groups of teachers discussed major and minor details that recurred every time the program was implemented. They talked about the location, equipment, materials, and activities, none of which changed from year to year.

Skyland teachers claimed that report cards changed each year. When she was asked whether the report cards matched the curriculum, one teacher said, "I may have a difference of opinion. I question or dispute how one of these reads." When asked which items she disputed, she could not point one out and said, "It's OK." She added, "It was totally developed by the teachers.... Every year the report card is fine-tuned." The same teachers who debated the report card changes noted that the district is moving toward portfolio assessment. Another teacher said, "How can a report card like this work when so many people do not follow the curriculum and we cannot force them to do it?"

The researcher found no evidence that the report cards match the curriculum. When teachers were asked if they had a curriculum, they pointed to sets of books on shelves, desks, or cabinets, to indicate that they did. Teachers claimed to use the curricula for planning; but during the study, not one curriculum binder showed evidence of use.

Teachers protected the schedule because it provided time for planning and preparation for instruction. Over the past 4 years, teachers have negotiated blocks of planning time during the students' school day: seven early release days per year; ½ day each month for CTC (group planning time); 1 hour each day for preparation; 1 additional hour each week for preparation; 1 hour each week for health education, allowing 1 hour for preparation; 2 hours each week for specials (art, music, and two physical education classes per week); and release time for playground, noon duty, in-service, and special activities. The researcher calculated, based on one teacher's schedule, that the individual was engaged in teaching 180 minutes—3 hours—per day.

On a day when a special school activity was scheduled, two teachers were angry. One said, "Why wasn't [it] scheduled in the morning? I am going to lose my PE class." The other said, "I don't get my additional prep." At a staff meeting, a major point on the agenda was ensuring that every teacher's students left the room for an equal number of specialty classes. When the principal was asked about the schedule and the amount of preparation time, she said, "You mean to tell me that they still feel they do not have enough time?" She was angry and said, "We have given them so much time the last 3 years; how could they feel that way?" The principal was aware that some teachers teach only 180 minutes a day.

Teachers controlled planning for activities that affected their classrooms: report cards, field trips, and invited guest speakers. One teacher claimed that the school has a handbook to guide school activities, but said she never used it. In the lounge a wall chart outlined the discipline plan for each grade level and level of offense. The researcher did not see teachers looking at or discussing the chart. When a teacher was questioned about the handbook and procedures, he said, "I just keep focused on where I am going."

Administration

Teachers accept administrators as decision-makers and support them when they share an educational vision. Teachers want the administration to facilitate their own visions by providing support and controlling other people, including other teachers, administrators, parents, and community members.

Dryden

Decision-Makers. Teachers differ in their opinions of the need for decisive administration. Administrative decisions that support the teachers are perceived as helpful. A teacher said, "That's who we go to. We give suggestions and they make the final decisions." Another said, "The extra support means a lot to a teacher. Sometimes it is good to be forced into change, in this case [restructuring] was a good change." Another teacher saw the administration as a means to control parents. She said, "Parents have too much control.... He has changed that." But a teacher who did not like a decision commented, "[The former principal] said I could cry, scream, and yell, but [the decision] was not going to change."

Support. The administrative staff was moved to a separate building during the restructuring, and as a result, a superintendent/principal was assigned to the building. Teachers complained that he was not available for support because his duties took him out of the building. A teacher said, "We need someone to deal with the day-to-day problems that take persistence to solve." Another teacher

said, "If things don't improve, like discipline, I need to know [the superinten-
dent/principal] is going to back me." Observation verified that the superinten-
dent/principal was out of the building 50% of the time. If problems that required
administrative action developed when he was out the office, the secretary made
decisions with one of two aides. A teacher questioned about this practice said,
"It makes it hard to know what to do."

Elkin

Decision-Makers. Teachers differ in their perceptions of the principal as
decision-maker. One teacher explained that when she needed time off from
school, the principal helped draft a request to the board. She said, "[The
principal] is by the book." Another teacher feels the principal should take more
active control of the school. "He should know what is going on. If it is not, he
should make it go on. The principal should be in the classroom and not selling
tickets."

Teachers report liking the principal. A regular education teacher said, "You
could not ask for a better person here. He identifies the problem, offers more
than one solution, and we decide the direction." A special education teacher said,
"I like him, but he doesn't take a stand; not everyone likes that."

Support. Teachers perceive the principal as supportive. They say he is
available to them and provides professional support. A special education teacher
said, "He is a workaholic. He is here at 5:00 in the morning and stays until
midnight." A regular education teacher said, "[He] works much too hard and is
very supportive of teachers wanting to try new things. I feel very safe with what
I try." Teachers report the principal supports them while helping to solve
problems with parents. A teacher said, "I had one parent that yelled at me for
disciplining a student.... I went down and told the principal. Having support from
the principal is important." A teacher who has changed schools four times said,
"I keep moving to find a principal I can work with." She explained that this
principal is supportive and she likes teaching at this school.

Skyland

Decision-Makers. Teachers like the administration's decision-making
role when decisions are aligned with their beliefs, protect them, and force others
to conform. One teacher said, "Teachers want the administration involved for
protection.... Some thought it would be OK if the change worked out, if not then
it was the administration's problem." A specialty teacher said, "A lot comes from
the principal, she believes in a team spirit. We are all important. The leader must
have a vision to go there." A split-grade-level teacher views the administration's
power as a means to provide for needs. She said, "...help get in-services and

support people in making changes.... The superintendent is all that and more. Our building principal is far and away the best principal I have worked with."

Most teachers perceive the administration's management style as collaborative. In only one instance, a teacher said the administration should take a dictatorial role. This teacher wanted an individual to conform to her ideas. A team of teachers was planning a grade-level activity. A specialty teacher said, "I do not want to be assigned to a group. I need to go where the kids need me." After the specialty teacher left the room, one teacher said, "If [that individual] is going to be there, she is being assigned to a group.... We should just have [the principal] tell her she is going to do it." The next day the specialty teacher was assigned to a group. She did not want to talk with the researcher about the assignment.

Support. Teachers perceive the Skyland administration as supportive, and are afraid that they will lose this support. One teacher said, "The administration will support us. My fear is we are going to lose some good administrators. They have been targeted by the [conservative] group. The group believes if they get rid of the administration, they will have their way." Another teacher said, "[The administrators] spend a lot of time justifying the changes we are making."

Teachers with innovative programs say that the administration supports their programs. When asked if she was concerned about her program being dropped, one teacher said, "I am not concerned, the superintendent and principal think it is a good program." Two other teachers with similar programs made the same claim.

Teachers who do not support the changes being carried out in the school did not report administrative support. A teacher who backed the conservative group said, "[An administrator] was involved in the SEC [School Evaluation Consortium] review. I have to think about how. We had questions and concerns for her. I don't remember how she supported us." The same teachers claimed that the principal was not dealing with the discipline problems in the school.

Conflicting Needs: School and Home

Teachers report constantly being pulled in many directions. The time-management choices they make create conflicts between their professional and personal lives. It appeared that most teachers valued certified support services and support staff, as essential to their own work, to counterbalance conflicting needs. In Dryden and Skyland, teachers have lost support services and are trying to obtain support staff. In Elkin, teachers reported no concerns about the need for support staff; evidence suggests that their needs were met. However, teachers could not say how these services improved student learning. They seemed to value support services that help them carry out their work or give them additional planning time. In addition, support services may help to reduce the stress teachers feel from balancing their professional and personal lives. Observation suggests that support services provided by educational assistants may be a status issue for some teachers.

Dryden

Teachers believe that certified support services and support staff help the school give more to students. They reported that the following positions had been reduced: guidance and counseling, a school social worker, a gifted and talented coordinator, and exceptional educational need services. A teacher commented on the effects of these losses: "The board wants everything to remain the same with less people, which has resulted in less support for teachers. That relates to the self-preservation, it becomes the survival of the fittest."

Teachers said the reduction in aide (educational assistance) time had a negative effect on their ability to improve student learning. A first-grade teacher said, "If I had more I could do more." She says she has more administrative work to do, because of the reduction in aide time. However, when teachers were asked what additional things they would do with more time, they did not give specific or direct answers. One teacher said, "The school hired a social worker half time. It was wonderful." She was asked, "How does this help?" She responded, "This helped with communications with the parents." No teacher suggested that additional support time would improve student learning.

Teachers perceive general bookkeeping as interfering with the instructional process. A kindergarten teacher complained about the time lost each day to helping students with lunch money and sending students to the office for medications.

Professionally, teachers want to do more for students, but using the new methods of teaching takes more time. A teacher who supports OBE said, "In philosophy it's a good program. Realistically it is a lot of paperwork." A teacher opposed to OBE confirmed this: "Time rules all. You must get it done."

The conflicting demands of job and family create feelings of guilt and health problems. A teacher said, "You are always pulled between your job and family. I go home and I don't have any more energy and time to spend on them. Working me and home me, it's the real me that says, God I am tired." Another teacher said, "Some teachers are resentful they have to work and leave their kids home." Two teachers with children at home agreed. One said, "I feel guilty about being here and having my kids at home." Other teachers talked about struggles with divorce, health problems, and their children. All teachers appear to share the common problem of being both a professional and a family person.

Elkin

Support services provided by certified staff and educational assistants have increased over time. Teachers did not raise concerns about support services during their interviews; however, the Elkin principal reported that teachers had complained in the past about the lack of a guidance counselor, special education teachers, a reading specialist, and educational assistants. He said that teachers no longer request additional support services because "they do not have any extra duties any more." Apparently, staff added by the district in recent years have resolved the shortage teachers perceived.

Teachers report being pulled in many different directions. Teachers must choose how to use limited time, which often creates conflict between their professional and personal lives. A teacher with 20 years in the district said, "I feel like teaching is a 24-hour-a-day job and you never really leave it, not even during the summer." A teacher with 10 years' experience said, "Sometimes we are bombarded with so many requests and responsibilities from so many different angles, it is...overwhelming. Too many little groups that want teachers to do too many things and they are not always compatible." Another teacher commented, "There is a lot of time spent on paperwork and committees." This creates a problem for some teachers: "It's a time factor for teachers. Teachers do have their own families. With all the committee work, time is not left for families." One teacher summed up: "The problem is you are torn; many of the things do seem valuable."

Skyland

Teachers talked about the positive effects of one person who provides support service, and were indifferent to others. The individual whom teachers like has influenced the administration to make changes that move instruction outside the classroom. Teachers believe that the new programs have improved instruction and given them more freedom. A teacher commented on other support services: "I regard aides as imperative. I feel lucky not to have playground or lunch duties." When the researcher probed for information on certified support services, he received none.

Teachers are pulled in many different directions and must choose how to use their time. A teacher concerned about teacher burnout said, "Teachers try to be too many things to too many people. You're working with kids and it is personal. It takes a lot of emotional energy." A specialty teacher said that her time choices were affected by "the realization of how much time it takes to get where [administrators] want you to go and the time it takes to get there." A split-grade-level teacher said, "You could be a teacher 24 hours a day and weekends. It is hard to separate your family life from the career. It is not a 9-to-5 job." A classroom teacher added, "You lose your personal life, because you work so hard. You keep giving more and more. You have to put your foot down and say 'no more.' Regardless if I am getting paid for the duty or not." A special education teacher commented, "I and my fiancée are going to be teachers all our lives. We always planned to be teachers and there will not be time to have people over to our house. As teachers we just don't have time to interact with other people."

Other School Services

In general, teachers speak positively about their buildings, transportation, and food service. Most teachers claim these services do not affect them. When teachers provided negative reports, they focused on specific past issues, which usually had been resolved. In Dryden, teachers reported two unresolved problems that interfered with the instructional program. One involved a change in a specific service for a classroom. The second involved an individual who adjusted a work schedule to favor a few teachers. In general, the data suggest that if system services do not conflict with the instructional programs, and do not affect teachers' status, teachers remain unconcerned.

Dryden

When teachers were asked, "Does your school building affect you as a teacher?" they generally reported that they had a great janitorial staff who kept the building clean. A teacher said, "The cleaning is good. It does not bother me. It would if it wasn't." A certified special teacher said, "When I started teaching I had a safe clean place for kids. This is not the case in this district." He explained that the building does not get cleaned if it is used by the public after school. However, the janitorial staff's activity contradicts this statement. Building cleaning starts at 6:00 AM, so the area the teacher used was cleaned every morning, after any public evening use.

Building maintenance affected teachers differently, depending on whether repairs were completed after one written request. The head of maintenance was under pressure from the administration, board of education, and the public to keep the buildings in good repair; but he was controlled by his budget. The researcher observed that repairs were made when they would be visible to the public or important to teachers who had administrative or parent support. Other repairs were given low priority. For example, over a 2-month period, two different people sent a total of five work orders for repair of the public address system. The repair was not completed until a person close to the administration filed a written request. A broken window with missing glass was not in public view, and was in the room of a low-status teacher. The window was broken before the researcher began work in the school and, although two work orders had been filed and personal contact made with the head of maintenance, the window had not been repaired by the time the researcher left the school months later. Repairs visible to the public were repaired without written requests; these included plugged sewers, graffiti, broken doors, and faulty tables.

Teachers commonly complained about lack of storage space. A teacher said, "If storage does not improve, that is a stress factor. I have a storage problem. I have to have things ready on my impulse." The researcher found that each classroom had shelves that covered most of the wall space and were used as dividers. The shelves were filled with books, boxes of instructional supplies, and other instructional materials; many were dusty. Teachers were asked, "Why do you have so many materials?" A teacher responded, "You do not know when the next change will come. I need these materials so I am ready."

No one voluntarily mentioned problems with the bell system, but observation suggested that the types of bells and their volume created confusion and interruptions. Teachers who were asked to explain what the different types of bells meant did not know. They reported using only the starting and ending of school bells. The office secretary knew what the bells were for and the schedule the bells supported, but she reported that the bell system is not accurate. So it is used only to keep rough time.

Teachers reported problems with busing when the school was restructured. One teacher said, "There are three types: red, blue, and green. It was very confusing." She felt that early problems with the transportation had been resolved. She and other teachers reported using class time to help students get on the correct bus. A teacher who did not support the restructuring said, "Some kids have long rides on the buses, more than an hour. Some kids don't get breakfast." The researcher found that the longest bus ride any child had was 1 hour, and the school's food service sold breakfast foods before school. During observation, kids were well behaved and entered the correct buses without assistance.

Teachers boycotted the food service at the beginning of the year when, to save money, it switched from paper milk containers to plastic pouches. Teachers in the lounge claimed that the new bags are difficult for students to handle. During the morning and afternoon milk breaks in the classroom, the bags leak if they are placed sideways on the slanted surface of a desk. Teachers must then help students clean up the spill. One teacher also noted, with the plastic pouches, "We don't have milk cartons for Easter projects."

Elkin

Teachers felt that the building is kept clean, and they get adequate help moving heavy objects, but they reported problems with maintenance. A teacher with more than 20 years in the building said, "It is important. The quality of the building is how you feel about being in the building. Polished floors, things are fixed and desks don't squeak. Our person is very good and willing to help build and move things." Observation confirmed her statement.

Teachers perceived building maintenance as good, but teachers did report maintenance problems that affect student learning. A special education teacher said, "Our roof leaks and the basement is flooded." Another teacher said, "I remember a roof repair was started one day after school started, which caused problems with noise. And an entry door was not fixed…. The…room is cold at times." A teacher reported, "My room is too hot. I cannot keep plants or animals."

And a special education teacher said, "One part of the building is ice-cold, kids have to wear coats."

Asked about these teachers' concerns, the superintendent said, "The building was built on an open concept. The teachers asked to have walls put up, which caused uneven heat. We would correct the problem if we knew how." The head of maintenance claims the district needs to hire help from outside the district to solve the problem. He said, "I don't have the money in the budget, we have other problems higher on the priority list."

Elkin teachers schedule transportation for field trips. They do not view student transportation to school as a current problem. The principal reports that, in the past, teachers complained about buses arriving early and students coming into their rooms, interfering with teachers' preparation time. The principal established a schedule that requires students to stay outside, or in the cafeteria during inclement weather, until 5 minutes before school starts. The principal claims teachers no longer complain of lost prep time.

A second-grade teacher said, "We have a wonderful food service program." Other teachers reported that food service had no effect on them. A first-grade teacher agreed that the school has good food service, but criticized what she called the state's procedures for serving food. "The state sets up how the program will run," she said. "All the teachers bring the students to the lunch room. We have to help them dish things out. We move from the role of the teacher to waitress.... This process causes the student to take more time than needed to get lunch." However, the researcher saw teachers drop off the students in a long lunch line, where an educational assistant watched them. Elkin teachers were not observed dishing out food.

Skyland

When asked, teachers made positive comments about the maintenance and operation of the building. "We have a wonderful building." "The building is always clean." "We have a great janitor, he will help us with anything." Observation confirmed teachers' reports. The building is spotless: Floors are waxed; walls are painted or washed; windows are clean; the walls, doors, and furniture are free of marks. One day, teachers complained about the lack of heat in the building; the next day, the problem was solved.

Teachers did comment on the building's lack of rooms to accommodate inclement weather and teachers' needs. One teacher said, "When it rains, this disrupts the [large room, for] the social studies program." He said, "The room is used for rainy day recesses, leaving the teachers scrambling to modify their plans." Another teacher said, "There needs to be a place where teachers can work without being disturbed.... On CTC [group planning time] days...teachers can never keep a room for the entire time of the meeting...we are always getting kicked out and moved." A third teacher said, "Teachers need a place where they can go and blow off steam. A safe place to talk and be yourself and say what is needed.... So everything is not always discussed."

Only one teacher responded to a set of open-ended questions about transportation. She reported that students had lost instructional time when they walked from the elementary school to another building for special program instruction. After she reported the problem to the principal, the children were transported by bus.

The researcher probed for information about the effects of the food service on teachers or school operations, and received no input.

SUMMARY/COMMENT

Several authors argue that schools lack a method (process) to plan school improvements (Deming, 1993; Rankin, 1992; Lezotte, 1990b; Purkey and Smith, 1985). This study supports their conclusions. The schools studied do not have policies that establish how improvements will occur; however, each school's administration did attempt to use a formal strategic planning method to establish a clear school mission. This study suggests that if a written plan existed for planning improvement, it would be subject to political forces. In each subject school plans for change were developed based on interactions between the formal and informal leadership's use of power and influence.

Lezotte (1992a,b) and Purkey and Smith (1985) argue that school policies and rules are designed to control teachers. The data support this claim. Although the subject schools had detailed policies outlining rules and procedures, these were seldom used or followed by teachers. The open practice of not following written procedures that conflict with a teacher's vision allows individuals and small groups to reframe the rules to protect themselves.

CHAPTER 11

Perception or Reality

INTRODUCTION

Groups and individuals compare the results attained by an organization with their own visions of success. This comparison is what makes people decide whether or not to take action. Whether the results are real or perceived is not the point. In the current system, individuals generally use gut feelings, rather than data, to evaluate results, and do not consider whether poor results have been produced by special cause or common cause problems. In some of the examples we've considered, people have treated special cause problems as common cause, and vice versa (see Chapter 3). This practice seems to promote the political power structure, and as a result, gut feelings about results are affected by the political climate of the day.

This problem is made worse by the misuse or inconsistent use of data. Some groups and individuals have used disconnected data or the results of evaluation tools, such as state tests, to promote their visions of good schools and classrooms. As will be shown in this chapter, these practices drive fear into the organization and further promote the inconsistent use—or misuse—of data.

The improper evaluation of results by relying on gut feelings, misusing data, and failing to distinguish between common cause and special cause problems all allow the political power structure to maintain an unstable system. Such a system lacks both a common vision and procedures to solve problems, and this enables the informal leadership to control the organization in a way that it safely maintains or enhances leadership's own vision of a good school or classroom. As problems cycle through the system, the internal culture learns not to take risks, because changes pay few dividends and failure is devastating. Teachers protect, maintain, or enhance their visions by attempting to create favorable images of themselves or their school.

We will look at the results dimension of the system by considering three general categories (use of data, evaluation of instruction, and cultural beliefs) that explain why teachers back evaluations that the data do not support. Each category will examine the three school systems (Dryden, Elkin, and Skyland).

RESULTS DIMENSION

Use of Data

Interviewees in each subject school related stories of teachers having been harmed through the misuse of data. In Dryden, teachers and others confirmed that a reading specialist used data to rank teachers and coerce them to change their teaching methods. In Elkin, the local newspaper editor used biased, irrelevant data to make a debatable point. The newest member of the board cited the editor's conclusion without understanding what the data measured. In Skyland, teachers talked about the third-grade reading test and cited another school in the district where parents were angry with the test scores and caused problems for the teachers and the principal. In each school high scores seemed to have little impact on the image of the school or a teacher, but low scores created a perception that the school or teacher was not doing a good job. High test scores do not provide a big reward, and low test scores represent high risk.

Skyland teacher evaluations were void of data on student learning. Teachers in the subject schools were not concerned about teacher evaluations unless the principal made a negative comment in the evaluation. Teachers perceived administrative evaluations as ephemeral, which suggests that evaluations have minimal effects on the teachers' visions. In Skyland, teacher evaluations by administrators did not affect the social structure or threaten the teacher's vision, but informal evaluations by parents and community members did concern teachers.

Dryden

Teachers feel pressured by the collection of test data for outcome-based education (OBE). A teacher said, "I teach both [OBE and her old program] because, not because we like them, but because we have to. The results are sent to the computer." Another teacher commented, "We're forced to do it. Some people fake it." The former principal agreed with these teachers: "Now we are putting more pressure on them." She said the teachers think the data are sent to the board of education.

Two teachers and the former principal were in agreement about the misuse of data by a former reading specialist. They claimed she used the data to pressure teachers into changing their classroom teaching; that she was dishonest when she gave teachers information; and that she used the data to rate teachers when she reported test results to the board. This occurred 10 years ago, but the teachers and principal still remember the fear it created among the staff. A board member confirmed the story, saying that he remembered the person and that her reports did rate teachers.

Teacher Evaluations. Formal teacher evaluations are not common in Dryden, and teachers consider them a minor inconvenience. One teacher commented on when evaluations occur, she said, "They never do. I cannot remember the last time." She thought it might have been 4 years ago. Another teacher said, "The administration evaluates me. It is not a problem. I only feel accountable to my kids." Other teachers report similar time lines and discount the importance of administrative evaluations.

Informal evaluation does concern the teachers. One said, "Voices in the community get to the school board with inaccurate information. Then the board uses it to come down on teachers." Board members feel differently: "I don't know why there is an issue of security," one said. "Teachers cannot be fired unless they break the law. Two teachers were fired from the district [in 10 years]; one was a starting teacher and the other broke the law." The former principal of the school felt a workshop on OBE caused the teachers' fear. The teacher who attended brought back the message, "If your students do not perform well on the OBE test, the district will fire you." This message was based on the actions of a board in New York State. There teachers were fired when their students' performance was below standard.

Elkin

Teachers and administrators limit their use of data. Teachers use data to grade students; each teacher keeps a record book of students' work. Teachers who use the whole group method struggle with how to grade students individually. One teacher said, "I walk around when the students are in groups and give individual grades for the group work. I don't believe in giving the group a grade. Some students contribute; others do not." One teacher argued against the use of a bell curve. She said, "If you use the bell curve, some kids have to fail. All the kids should meet the objective." The principal said, "The biggest issue right now is the assessment. We don't know if portfolios, writing, or tests are the way to go. We just don't know, but it should be consistent." One concerned teacher said, "We have made all kinds of changes, but we never research to find out how we did. We never look at the data."

Teacher Evaluations. Teachers are not concerned about evaluations by the principal. When teachers were asked, "How do evaluations affect you?" only two teachers offered any information other than saying, "They don't." One teacher, Kathy E1, said, "We have them, I think it does, I am not uncomfortable with him coming in. I am past that, but it used to be. The saliva would dry in my mouth. I was afraid [a student] would misbehave." Another teacher said, "They made me feel good, but I could have used more suggestions. I could have used more things to improve."

Skyland

Teachers and administrators have limited use for data. Teachers collect data on individual students and record the results in a grade book. The data are converted into a grade, showing degree of mastery, as dictated by the report card standards. Teachers were asked whether they used the information to compare groups of students from different years. One teacher said, "I collect different data each year." Another said, "I cannot use it for that. Each year kids are different." Teachers are working toward the use of portfolios to report student progress; however, they could not state what end results they expected.

The administration claims that teachers are concerned that data collected by the school are public information. The principal said, "I would like to see teachers trained in the use of data. Teachers go nuts when they know that data is being collected. Anytime you collect data teachers seem to think it is public information."

In general, use of data focuses on particular problems important to administrators and teachers. The superintendent looks at the progress of site-based management (SBM); the principal focuses on discipline, teachers on control of their classrooms.

When one teacher expressed concern because local businesses criticized the educational system, the researcher followed up her comments by role-playing: "Suppose I am a businessman or a manufacturer and I say that schools have been given all kinds of money." The researcher cited former Governor Earl's commitment to funding education. "A lot of dollars were given to schools and student learning did not improve. How do you defend that?" The teacher argued, "A lot of people say that, but the story is never backed with data or documents." The researcher asked, "What about the documents [state reports] that say schools are not doing a good job? Earlier you stated that you did not have data to support your conclusion that students did learn more in your class now than 4 years ago. You claim they do not have data, but are you requesting the same from them—they should go on faith, but your comments are believable?" She said, "I agree, but I do not know how to collect data." It appeared that both this teacher and the businesspeople based their conclusions on "gut feelings". The teacher claimed not to know how to collect data, and businesspeople's ability to use data was questioned.

Teacher Evaluations. Skyland teachers varied in their level of concern about the evaluation of their work. The principal said she evaluated each teacher once a year. One group of teachers looked forward to the evaluation; another group was not concerned. A teacher new to the school was in the office on the day of his first evaluation by the principal. He said, "I am looking forward to it.... This is an important day...for feedback." A specialty teacher with more than 15 years in the district said, "We have a good evaluation system. No one gets too upset. When [administrators are] here, you feel it a little; after it's over you forget it." A teacher with 5 years in the district said, "They come and go. It is only an issue when the time is there." A 20-year district veteran said, "My evaluations are good. I don't worry about them." The researcher asked, "Aren't the evaluations based on perception?" She looked at the researcher and said, "I guess; well, I don't know."

Other Skyland teachers believe that evaluations are based on set goals and perceptions. A teacher with more than 15 years in the district was asked, "What are teachers' evaluations currently based on?" She said, "How I am reaching the goals of the school site. How do I interact with children. Observation of my class and to a certain degree a finished product." The researcher asked, "How are the goals set?" She said, "We set a goal and then the principal would evaluate me on the completed project.... I also believe from experience, a lot of observations are based on the class and if the students are under control, or if there are complaints from parents or other teachers."

Another teacher discussed her fear of the goals determined by the requirements for charter schools. (Such schools are released from standard state regulations in order to promote innovations). She was concerned that if a teacher did not meet the goals, the parents and community would say she was a bad teacher.

One teacher argued that portfolios would support student learning. When the researcher raised the issue of teacher performance, she said that no one evaluates teachers and added, "I don't know how you would evaluate teachers' teaching."

Evaluation of Instruction

Use of data varied in each school system, so it was not surprising to find that data collection was inconsistent and data were not analyzed. In addition, some teachers claimed they lacked training in how to use the data. On the other hand, some teachers and administrators claim they use data to defend the schools instructional program. This suggests that data to evaluate may not be used for instructional improvement, but may be rejected or used to create a perception of how well students are learning.

Dryden

Existing data for evaluating student learning are unreliable. A teacher with more than 20 years in the school district said, "Testing in the district is inconsistent. We had CTBSs [Comprehensive Test of Basic Skills] in third and fourth grades. Then we tested every grade level...then reduced it...as time and money became an issue.... Now the district is starting IQ tests.... We see the pendulum move back and forth." It was impossible to verify this teacher's comment because neither teachers, administrators, nor office staff knew where the old records were. It seemed that administration, teachers, and others were not concerned the records were missing.

The Dryden district was currently collecting test data to support OBE. Teachers considered the process complete if all students have mastered the particular competency being tested. The teachers report test results to the office, where office staff are supposed to enter the data and develop reports. However, the office has not followed through with the evaluation; staff is behind on data entry. Reports indicate which children have passed the tests, but no other use of the data was observed.

The administration is installing a database to track students' progress, but only one teacher reported knowing of the program. When other teachers were asked about the database, they said they'd heard the name of the software, but could not explain its purpose.

Despite observations and interviews, the researcher could not discover where data analysis was done. Teachers reported that data from national normed tests and state tests were distributed. They said they looked at the reports, but did not use them for planning. Three teachers were asked how they analyzed data. They said they did not know how to compare classes that took the same test. One teacher said, "You cannot compare one year's class to another, because of the variation in students." She believed this was true even if the classes took the same test.

Elkin

The data for evaluating student learning are inconsistent. The Elkin direc-tor of curriculum said, "We have results on standardized tests for 5th, 8th, and 10th grade, the 3rd-grade reading test, and the end-of-the-year kindergarten test. Now we have the state's 8th- and 10th-grade test.... We also have the ACT scores [college entrance exam]. In the elementary it [testing] is not consistent. There are the teachers' self-developed test." The principal said, "The district used to give a lot of tests, but it was not consistent. A different test was used each year.... The school contracted with test companies that had booths at... conventions. The district moved to the state test for 5 years to meet the requirements of the Twenty Standards. Now the state has dropped the tests." For the past 6 years, the district has administered the state's third-grade reading test and a national normed-stand-ardized test in fifth grade, in all schools. But other data are inconsistent. The reading specialist said, "Testing is not consistent in the district.... I heard tests were dropped in fifth grade." Generally, teachers do not talk about data, because, as one teacher said, "We don't have data."

A testing program accompanied the new textbooks for whole language instruction. One teacher reported using the tests for spelling. She said, "This made more problems for both low and high students.... I used to have an individualized spelling program.... This was difficult...the textbook company set the standards for spelling." Another teacher talked about her personal records:

"I do not keep similar data from one year to the next. I don't believe it is necessary."

When the principal was asked where test results were kept, he pointed to a file cabinet. He has records in his desk for the third and fifth grades, but data from past testing programs remain in the file, unused.

The researcher could not learn where test data were analyzed or distributed for interpretation. One teacher said, "We never look at the data." A fifth-grade teacher said, "The only parts of the tests that are looked at are the low areas. I don't believe formal analysis is done." The principal reported reviewing the composite scores for the third-grade reading test and a norm-referenced fifth-grade test. He said he talked to the teachers about the test scores. The superintendent reviewed SAT scores, dropout rates, and data from new programs that had been implemented. He used the data to defend the school district against attacks for poor performance.

The director of instruction said, "Really, standardized tests are only one day out of the lives of the students." The researcher probed for more information. She said, "You cannot use the data from one year to the next because the students vary from one year to the next." The researcher questioned her about analysis of variance [statistical test used to determine the degree of difference between groups], which does what the director of instruction claimed could not be done; but she did not respond.

Skyland

The data evaluating Skyland students' learning are inconsistent. The superintendent said, "In the area of testing we are at ground zero. We have started to develop a test in math...." A teacher with more than 20 years in the district said, "Our testing program is inconsistent. We test for a while; then it is dropped for lack of money, or administration goes a different direction." The principal confirmed that test data are inconsistent, but she has the data for tests given in the last 3 years. Because of pressure from the conservative group these tests may be changed or dropped.

Teachers fear data will draw attention to their programs or classrooms. A teacher teaching a new program in the district said, "[Program] data —there is not data collected to focus attention on [the program]." A group of classroom teachers met with the principal to request dropping the testing for their grade level.

The researcher found no evidence of data analysis, and administration and teachers confirmed that data are not analyzed. The principal defends the changes carried out in the school, but she said, "I do not have data to compare one year to the next, or over time." A specialty teacher said, "We give the [test] now. They are not going to score them.... The school is giving a very old test...it is scored by hand and never sent to the company for detailed analysis." She was not sure whether all of the tests were scored.

Teachers said they were not trained to analyze data. One teacher claims that data are not analyzed for the general student population but are used to identify students with special needs. Another said, "I don't have anything [data analysis] that shows that [student progress] over time. It would be so hard to compare [previous year's students to the next], because student groups are different. They learn different ways."

Cultural Beliefs

It is not surprising that none of the three schools produce measurable results. The political structures place little value on data. Classroom teachers, administrators, and board of education members have more faith in their perceptions of good education than in numeric data. That is, each system promotes perception as a means of evaluation. People in each school told stories about the inappropriate use of data to force, dominate, or manipulate teachers' behavior. This created fear and caused teachers to change their methods of instruction so as not to be labeled as a poor teacher; not surprisingly, teachers protected themselves with evaluation methods based on perceptions that are not easily quantified, such as portfolios.

When the political structure forces teachers and/or schools to use quantitative measures, teachers act to minimize negative results that could affect their power or status. For example, subject schools ensured that scores on the third-grade reading test met the expectations of parents, community members, and administrators.

Special education teachers represent "an exception that proves the rule": they use data eagerly and correctly because their culture values individual student assessment based on data. The use of data by special education teachers to show parents how their child improved seems to increase the teacher's status.

Administrators used methods similar to those chosen by teachers to protect themselves from the political system. Administrators evaluated school performance with self-selected measures that correlated with news media measures. In each school, administrators used selected data to demonstrate that their school was doing well compared with others. However, administrators' most important measures of school success focused on issues other than student learning: cost, dropout rates, number of programs offered, and discipline.

Board members based their evaluations of school and teacher performance on their own views of education, information obtained by contacts with parents and community members, and news media coverage of the school. Teachers in each school reported concerns about being evaluated by board members on hearsay information.

This study suggests that when data are available, people have misused them; therefore, teachers protect themselves by downplaying the value of data, ensuring that data present a favorable image of them and their school, and creating evaluation methods that build or maintain their status. By controlling the perceptions held by parents, community members, and administrators, teachers protect their social rank, which protects their vision of a school.

Dryden

Classroom Teachers. When classroom teachers were asked, "How do you know you are doing a good job?" they judged their teaching effectiveness via their own perceptions. The following conversation with a teacher who has 25 years in the district is representative of responses from other teachers.

RESEARCHER: How do you know you are doing a good job?

TEACHER: Accountability.

R: Accountability? What is that?

T: From a teacher to student, making sure that the students learned the minimum and check that they have learned.

R: How do teachers check that?

T: You're constantly checking that, you question, you talk to the students, and you keep that in your head.

R: How do you know you're doing a better job this year than last?

T: It depends on the kids. A teacher takes a child as far as [she or he] can, then the next person gets them.

R: How do you know you are doing a better job now than 5 years ago?

T: [Thinks for a while.] I could demonstrate that.

R: How would you do that?

T: I could not defend my position with data.

Other teachers, asked similar questions, reported knowing they were doing a good job by their feelings or by comments from others. A teacher said, "I see the kids smiling and exploring learning. They get excited about something new. Parents ask to have their children in my room. I can feel if I am doing a good job." Other teachers replied: "From parents' and teachers' feedback." "The administration tells me." "I compare myself to other teachers."

Other teachers, asked whether they had improved over the last 5 years, said, "I don't know." One teacher added, "Not without tests." The researcher asked a teacher known to be upset and concerned over the constant change that had taken place in Dryden, "How do you know you have improved?" She flared up: "I have never gotten a demand for improvement. I have gotten a demand for change." Her point was supported by observations.

Special Education Teachers. Special education teachers share a view of the improvement of student learning that differs from the classroom teachers'. Two special education teachers noted, "Kids have IEPs [individualized educational plans] so we have a different measure." Each special education teacher claims to look at the IEP, reviewing the document and comparing it with daily progress reports kept on each student. When asked about other measures, they report methods similar to those of classroom teachers. One teacher said she knows she is doing a good job "long term, if the parents are happy and administration tells me, and my peers tell me." Asked if they were doing a better job now than 5 years ago, special education teachers responded, "I would have to look at the IEPs." They could not confirm improvement without reviewing their records, but claimed they would know.

Others. Dryden administrators were asked similar questions about evaluation. The former principal said, "I don't know about this year, [but] fifth and sixth [graders] are more ready than in the past to advance." She agreed with the researcher that this was a "gut feeling." For her, school improvement meant better discipline and fewer parent complaints. The superintendent/principal said, "It's hard to compare apples to apples, we have no comparison. We have had a decrease in complaints about teachers and leadership to the board and administration." He claims the teachers feel the school has improved. He added, "When we set up plans for next year, it [decrease in parent and teacher complaints] will bear out if we have made improvements." A board member said, "The attitudes of the parents and teachers are a measure." When asked about other measures, he said, "A lot of my decisions were based on my own personal beliefs." Later in the interview he added, "The data that is available in the district is not valid to base decisions on." He was upset about not having measures to evaluate the school.

Elkin

Classroom Teachers. Regular classroom teachers judged student learning through their own perceptions and feedback from others. When teachers were asked, "How do you know if you are doing a better job this year than last year or 5 years ago?" the standard answer was, "I don't know." A teacher with 20 years in the district added, "Stop, the emperor has no clothes! We were doing a good job 5 and 10 years ago." Another 20-year veteran said, "By standardized tests? We only have a few. Objectively, you're making some improvements."

When Elkin teachers were asked, "How do you know you are doing a good job?" their answers varied. A teacher with 20 years in the district said, "I don't know how you would ever assess that. We implement programs on pure faith...."

Sometimes it just doesn't feel right when comparing [to] the old ways of doing things. I am supportive of whole group instruction, but I know other teachers do not feel comfortable with it." Other teachers view changing methods of teaching or adding equipment as school improvements. A teacher said, "We're improving the use of computers and using the Internet to study the different continents and countries." Another teacher said, "Through the teacher using new methods for instruction. It helps discipline problems, and [provides] new information on subjects."

Teachers who mentioned tests did not value them. A teacher with 20 years in the district said, "We used to test a lot and found the tests were not of much value on how we were doing. The children change and we don't have good measures." A specialty teacher said, "I view each student as an individual and do not compare the results of one student to another. Testing in groups is not a good way to diagnose student learning." One teacher was angry with the question related to evaluation. She said, "I have trouble with paper-and-pencil tests. I keep portfolios and pictures of students' work.... Control and responsibility. The community states, 'Why can't they be made to learn?' They do not focus on the school's successes. [Both] parents and students must be held responsible for learning."

Special Education Teachers. When special education teachers were asked how they knew whether they were doing a good job, or whether they had improved over the past year or 5 years, they cited IEPs to confirm the impact they had made on students. A special education teacher said, "Yes, I made plans based on my mistakes with the IEPs. This year I am writing objectives in terms the kids can understand... objectives are measurable and build on last year's IEPs. Data from individual students are compared one year to the next. I am improving by writing courses to improve the results on the IEPs. IEPs are helpful, but take a lot of time." Another special education teacher used IEPs in a similar manner.

Others. Elkin administrators were also asked about the evaluation of educational programs. The principal said, "We don't test enough to know how we are doing." He provided the researcher with data from a nationally normed, standardized test given in fifth grade, but said, "I hate to base a lot of things on testing." Then he explained that the fifth-grade teachers didn't take the test seriously, and do not follow approved testing procedures. He added that test scores were dropping until he talked to the teachers. "The next two years the test scores jumped dramatically [teachers reported teaching to the test]," he said. "Now their [Elkin's classroom test scores] are close to [those of another elementary school in the district]. [The other school's] test scores were high because they [teachers] exempt students from the test." The principal reported similar problems with the third-grade reading test.

The superintendent was sensitive to questions about evaluation. A recent editorial had attacked the school district because of declining test scores. The paper published the superintendent's rebuttal the next week, but printed it just in front of the ad section. The superintendent wrote: "We know we're improving through several measures. 1) The SAT scores...66% of our students took the test. We scored above the state average.... 2) We have fewer drop-outs than in the past.... 3) We have several more programs for special needs kids.... 4) We have never had a quantified way to say how we evaluated the past. It is in the eye of the beholder."

The researcher questioned Elkin board members about the editorial. They differed in their responses to the district's education program. One board member said, "The first perception is a misperception. We are going to go back and look at the strategic plan. We depend on the standardized test scores, we know that. Kids who don't score as high as they should require a remediation plan." The newest board member said, "You began with the assumption that the district is doing a good job. Our district has slipped terribly. I have asked teachers and administration where they think we rank in the state. The answers I receive are 75% to 65%." (When he attended school, he believed that the school district ranked in the top 10%.) "I don't know why that is. When I went to school it was geared to college prep.... I am curious if there is any hard data out there."

Skyland

Classroom Teachers. Regular classroom teachers use their own perceptions, as well as feedback from others, to evaluate student learning. A teacher with fewer than 10 years in the district, asked how she evaluates instructional programs, said, "The district may have records on some scores, or just may talk to teachers,... or interviewing parents. Or, observe the reaction of the parents and the children if they have been in the school for a long time." Another teacher said, "I have more confidence and experience...the students look forward to coming to class and are happy when they leave. The feedback is great now compared to 5 years ago. The principal, teachers, students, and parents are being positive." A teacher with 25 years in the district said, "I think the children [tell us], if the children are enjoying the activities and are verbally positive, I am doing OK." A teacher with more than 15 years' experience in teaching said, "I evaluate myself constantly. I am constantly asking three questions: (1) How did I do? (2) Would I do it again next year? (3) I evaluate myself all the time during the class. I watch how the children react to the instructions." A teacher with more than 25 years in the district said, "When you get into a slump, you end up getting mediocrity. Who knows, we're doing different things, but who knows?"

Other teachers said they use measures that will demonstrate whether the school or their teaching has improved. One teacher claimed that portfolios provide feedback: "Portfolios are better for long-term learning. Portfolios are better than pencil-and-paper tests, with fill-in-the-blank or multiple choice. These tests measure the information in a neat unit, not what the child can do over time." Other teachers liked to use portfolios to show parents what their children had done. When these teachers were questioned on how portfolios improve student learning, they focused on the parents rather than on the student. One teacher angrily said, "They show the parents what we have done. They will show progress over time."

A teacher who taught a special program said, "All the tests have produced excellent results.... You like to know you are doing a good job." When the teacher was asked for the test data, she said, "You will have to ask the special education people for that." But the special education people claimed not to know of any data related to the program. Another teacher who claimed to use data to evaluate student learning in her room was asked to share her records, but she declined.

Special Education Teachers. A special education teacher expressed concern about the classroom teachers' evaluation of student learning. She said, "Part of it is gut reaction. It depends on what is being tried. Is it proven, is it new, or do we need to change? A lot of it is collecting data on opinions. When communicating to parents you need to prove the benefits to get their support." This teacher was asked how she evaluates student learning. She said, "We get back to data. One way is the... test results...it needs to be concrete...so people can relate to it." She explained how IEPs are written each year, for each of her students. She reviews the IEPs and measures progress against test results at the beginning and end of the year.

Others. The superintendent said, "In the past the district scored in the top 5% on all tests.... It is hard to move [higher] on norm-referenced tests when you score that high. What we are doing is beefing up our assessment system.... Some of the areas we will see differences. I will not be measuring in student learning terms [that is, assessment will focus on the number of programs to benefit students], some [testing] will be done. It [student testing] will not be done as in other schools where the student is sacred [the only measure of the school's success]." When he was asked about measuring the variation in student learning within a single grade level, he said, "The new report card system will accommodate the variation," but would not elaborate.

The director of curriculum said, "We don't know. Schools are absolutely poor at collecting and analyzing data on students and learning. We always avoid measuring [at] the end, so we always measure the end [result] of the instructional program by if it [were well] implemented. What pushes us forward is a leap of faith that the new program will be better."

The principal said, "I can give you measures on discipline. I keep records on time, types, and who. Academically I keep records on reading in second and fifth grades. We use standardized tests. We have tests in fourth and fifth grade on math and reading and there is the third-grade reading test. We do not have any on students' attitudes. Personally, I keep a record of visits with teachers, parents, and notes I send to teachers." The researcher asked whether teachers allow students to practice the third-grade reading test. (A comment in the lounge suggested another school in the district administered a practice test.) The principal said, "We don't do anything that is not acceptable. It is OK to give the last year's test as a practice and find out who needs help on the test. We do that."

Board members criticized the evaluation processes used by the school. A liberal member of the old board said, "There are problems with the third-grade reading test. That test is a high-stakes test and schools will do everything possible within the limits of the test to score well." He knew that teachers gave pretests and worked with low-achieving children so they scored well. He added, "Special education students are written out of the test, which raises the overall test scores." He questioned the usefulness of norm- and criterion- referenced tests. He said, "We don't do any follow-up. In evaluation we do most things on myth and conjecture."

The new conservative board member similarly criticized the evaluation of student learning using existing data: "That is difficult to do, because of the validity of the test. On standardized tests we look good. The problem is defining success. We don't know the answer to 'what is success?'" He is concerned about the changes that have been implemented in the district. "It [the change] was not an improvement in the educational process. There was not proof that this would improve education and there still isn't." Both new board members believe the school district assesses changes based on gut feelings, and say that data do not prove that improvements have occurred. One new board member added, "This is why [teachers] want all the decisions based on perception and not on facts." Another board member believes the school has abandoned the purpose of education: "The restructuring used teachers', parents', and administrators' time while the academics were falling into a black hole. Now the school needs to put up or shut up about restructuring and get back to the purpose of school, which is to educate."

SUMMARY/COMMENT

This study supports Lezotte's (1992a) conclusion that teachers do not trust the use of data to monitor student progress. They are suspicious of how and why data are collected, generated, valued, and used. The findings also confirm Purkey and Smith's (1985) conclusion that teachers' fear of data evaluation— its frequent misuse—is well-founded. The schools studied based evaluations on individual perceptions of how closely aligned the program was to the local vision.

In addition, data were used to evaluate people, rather than the system. This practice is counterproductive, according to process improvement experts Deming (1993, 1986) and Juran (1992). They believe that people are doing their best and that placing blame or giving higher rewards will do little to improve results. It is the system, not people, that creates poor results. To improve results, the system must be improved.

None of the three schools currently use data to evaluate teacher performance. Data collected during interviews and observations suggest that in the past, data were used to control teachers, which created fear. This finding is consistent with that of Purkey and Smith (1985).

CONCLUSION

This book addresses the critical question of Chapter 1: Is the Teachers' Paradox real? Throughout the six organizational dimensions—external environment culture (Chapters 5 and 6), internal environment culture (Chapter 7), leadership (Chapter 8), strategy (Chapter 9), structure (Chapter 10), and results (Chapter 11)—findings confirm that the paradox does exist. It was not always perceived by teachers. Comments of teachers, support staff, administrators, board members, parents, and community members, taken as a whole and combined with direct observation, provided evidence of the paradox in all three of the subject schools. This is a paradox: teachers said they wanted to work in schools that focused on improving student learning; they reported using their time on self-preservation issues, namely, power, status, rewards, and well-being. (See Chapter 1.)

Why do teachers focus on self-preservation more than on improving student learning? The findings suggest that this question must be restated: Why do teachers assign a higher priority to their individual visions of how students should be educated than to more collective visions emerging from external mandates and administrative initiatives? The short answer is that schools are too politically driven and unstructured to offer teachers much choice.

The data suggest that every teacher wants to teach and to be the instrument through which children learn and improve, in accordance with the teacher's own vision. Teachers work hard to balance their individual visions against threats, and this constitutes the paradox.

The schools studied did not have a durable, real collective vision on which teachers could rely. Each subject school attempted to establish a collective vision; however, in each case the political structure of the environment or organization blocked the development or implementation of this vision. It seems reasonable to assume that teachers would place a higher priority on their own perceived stable vision than an unstable collective one.

The political system apparently causes teachers to protect the stability of their vision. Then relations with parents and community members represent a key variable. Without the support of parents and community members, teachers cannot maintain or develop stable visions for their classrooms. Within the organization, teachers use their informal power structure to maintain the stability of their visions when formal leadership attempts threatening or conflicting changes. The teachers' ability to protect their visions depends on their influence on the environment and their social rank within the school. When either is in jeopardy, teachers place a high priority on maintaining control. When they lose control, teachers place not only their vision, but themselves at risk, personally and professionally.

These findings support the existence of a paradox that appears to be created and promoted by the political system within which schools conduct their business.

CHAPTER 12

Thoughts on School Management

INTRODUCTION

Public officials and school administrators assume that changes they recommend will improve student learning. Teachers may be happy to make such changes. But as we've seen, teachers have quite different priorities. The teachers' priorities are a response to the instability of the school's mission, which results from diverse political agendas. Parents, community members, teachers, administrators, and others set their political agendas by comparing their own expectations of the school and its teachers to their perceptions of what the school does. This method of evaluation exacerbates the problem. The school's vision changes every time the political power structure changes. Because each change in the political power structure puts teachers at risk, they seek the relative safety of promoting their own visions of the school.

Teachers use power and influence to promote their own visions. They focus on actions that will build their power structure, because without a power structure, they lose control and may be forced to use methods contrary to their visions of good, child-centered instruction. Unless public officials and school administrators address the underlying causes of this paradoxical situation, teachers will continue to place higher priority on preserving their own visions than on implementing a collective vision that may improve student learning overall.

LITERATURE ON SCHOOL IMPROVEMENT

Innovations in schooling originate in many sources. Two research-based approaches to school improvement are the Effective Schools and the Deming models. Research on schools in which students learn more than is typical for poor or average schools led to the Effective Schools approach. Advocates of this approach argue that ordinary schools can improve student learning by copying key cultural characteristics and operating procedures found in effective schools (Lezotte, 1990a, 1987; Purkey and Smith, 1985, 1983).

The Deming approach is based on W. Edwards Deming's 14-point philosophy of management, which is a "customer"- or "stakeholder"-focused application of current theories on the behavior of systems. Deming also looks at causes of variation in system outcomes, psychology of human motivation, and knowledge creation. Advocates of the Deming approach argue that learning how to improve is something that administrators and teachers must discover through joint efforts. Together they identify and analyze causal relationships between the educational process and student outcomes. The Deming approach views educational process as a system whose purpose is to meet the valid need of external stakeholders. It uses a "scientific approach," learning to manage the organization as a system, developing process thinking, basing decisions on data, and understanding variation (Joiner, 1994, p. 11). The approach helps identify and eliminate causes of variation in system outcomes that prevent the system from meeting stakeholder (Chapters 5 and 6) needs. This, in turn, requires continuous efforts to train and motivate staff to improve the system and ultimately to satisfy its stakeholders (Stampen, 1992, 1994; Lezotte, 1992a; Glasser, 1990a,b).

Both the Effective Schools and Deming approaches can improve student learning (Bonstingl, 1993; Lezotte, 1992a, 1990b). The former focuses on transferring the best practices from one setting to another; the latter, on discovering from within how to improve a given school.

Apart from these approaches, many school districts have independently devised their own processes for improving schools., which this book calls this "self-developed approaches." Generally, the latter approaches to school improvement combine ideas and concepts from a variety of other approaches to innovation and change.

Conzemius (1993) investigated teacher attitudes in three otherwise similar types of public school districts in southern Wisconsin that had adopted different approaches to change: Effective Schools, Deming Schools, and Self-Developed Schools. His most important finding was that teachers in all three types of districts shared the same paradoxical view of school improvement. They all wanted their schools to focus on student learning. At the same time, however, they placed higher priority on conditions affecting their own employment, rewards, status, power, and well-being—which could cause them to downplay student-centered innovation.

Approaches to School Improvement

Effective Schools. Research on Effective Schools has used outlier studies (that is, comparing high standardized-test-scoring effective schools to low standardized-test-scoring ineffective schools) to identify differences between effective and ineffective schools. These studies found a set of characteristics common to effective schools, but not to ineffective schools. Research completed both in the United States (Cohn and Rossmiller, 1987; Lezotte, 1987; Purkey and Smith, 1985, 1983) and in developing countries (Hmaidan, 1991; Mohd Nor, 1989) produced similar results. These studies identified the following characteristics of effective schools:

- Effective schools have principals who communicate a clear mission of the school constantly and consistently and involve the teachers in the decision-making.
- Each effective school's climate is generally positive, and reflects high expectations for student success.
- Teachers in effective schools feel responsible for student learning, and frequently monitor student progress.
- Effective schools exist as safe, orderly environments where students learn without fear of harm, in a businesslike climate, and all staff believe they are always responsible for students while on duty at work.
- Effective schools offer opportunities for students to spend their time in learning activities based on an organized curriculum.
- Effective schools enjoy a high degree of parental and community involvement in deciding the school's mission.

In addition, Hmaidan, Mohd Nor, Cohn and Rossmiller, and Purkey and Smith specifically cite two characteristics of effective schools: a stable teaching staff, and organized staff development programs.

Many researchers agree that these characteristics are rooted in school culture and argue that duplication of the cultural characteristics found in effective schools will improve all schools. According to Purkey and Smith (1985), creating an effective school becomes a matter of altering a school's culture. To do this means changing school organization, school rules, and teachers' and principals' attitudes and behavior. The administration leads these changes by developing a sense of community, clear goals and high expectations, order and discipline, and collaborative planning.

Lezotte (1987) views school as having three missions: (1) teaching and learning (the most critical mission); (2) meeting students' safety and social needs; and (3) sorting and selecting students to fit into social, work, and educational categories. He argues that schools need to answer three questions before trying to adopt or change cultural characteristics to become effective: What is the mission of the school? What will you (the school and community) accept as evidence of school effectiveness? How will the school assess that evidence? Lezotte strongly believes that it is the combination of characteristics that make an effective school, and warns that focusing on only some of the characteristics may disrupt a school. "If schools are to implement the [desired cultural] characteristics," he cautions, "be prepared to take on all the characteristics at once."

The methods recommended by Lezotte and Purkey and Smith to implement the results of Effective Schools research rely on leadership that mandates or manipulates the organization to cause a cultural change.

Deming's Theory. Several educational researchers have reviewed Deming's theories of management [now known as Total Quality Management (TQM)]. They argue that TQM is suitable for adaptation to educational organizations (Bonstingl, 1993; McClanahan and Wicks, 1993; Lezotte, 1992a,b; Glasser, 1990a; Stampen, 1987). Deming developed his theories in reaction to "scientific management," incorporating ideas from several behavioral sciences into a new theory of systems management. Deming's theory assigns to management the responsibility for meeting the needs of both the external and internal customers of the organization.

The literature offers no model for systemwide implementation of the Deming approach in schools. However, the Deming approach has a highly developed theoretical foundation and highly developed procedures for planning and analysis. Improvement in organizational planning evolves through self-designed scientific approach innovations and incremental improvement between innovations. Deming advocates training people in ways to improve the system, creating a climate in which people want to participate, and helping people contribute their best efforts toward improvements.

Deming's Theory of Profound Knowledge is not a segmented theory. In *The New Economics: For Industry, Government, Education* (1993) Deming states, "The various segments of the system of profound knowledge cannot be separated" (p. 96). These segments include: (1) appreciation for system, (2) knowledge about variation, (3) theory of knowledge, and (4) psychology. A *system*, according to Deming, is "a network of interdependent components that work together to try to accomplish the aim of the system" (p. 50). *Knowledge about variation* informs management that there will always be variation among people in output, service, and product. By observing this variation, management can determine the capability of the processes necessary to carry out the aims of the organization. *Theory of knowledge* teaches that if a statement conveys knowledge, it will predict future outcomes, thus helping management to improve the processes that contribute to the aims of the organization. *Psychology* helps management understand individuals and interactions between individuals (including manager and subordinates, or teacher and pupils) in any system of management. In schools, the interaction among these four tenets of the Theory of Profound Knowledge guides administrators (the equivalent of management) in improving processes, thereby making it possible for teachers to improve student learning outcomes.

Deming provides a prescription called the 14 Points of Management to improve the organization of institutions. Vertiz, the director of the National Curriculum Audit Center, describes the fundamentals of Deming's theories for use in schools (Vertiz, 1992). She provides a brief description of the Theory of Profound Knowledge and a list of Deming's 14 Points to clarify his theory.

The literature reveals that the processes and tools within Deming's approach to quality management have improved schools. The most commonly used improvement processes are variations of the Plan–Do–Check–Act (PDCA) cycle which Deming (1993, 1986) outlines as a means of promoting continuous improvement. The PDCA cycle has been modified to provide a step-by-step procedure allowing schools to select a problem, identify and analyze the root cause of the problem, identify possible solutions, implement a solution, evaluate the results, and plan for greater improvements (Abernethy and Serfass, 1993; Kaufman and Hirumi, 1993; McClanahan and Wicks, 1993; Schmoker and Wilson, 1993; Audette and Algozzine, 1992; Bellanca, 1984).

A more sophisticated version of the PDCA approach, the House of Quality concept, adds surveys or other research to determine customers' needs. The steps used in building the House of Quality focus the organization on key issues for improvement. This allows the organization to conserve resources and better meet customer needs (Andrade and Ryley, 1993; Akao, 1990).

Analytical quality tools support the PDCA cycle. These tools help an organization determine what needs to be improved. The educational research literature describes how the use of Pareto charts, Ishikawa (fishbone) diagrams, cause-and-effect diagrams, matrices, tree diagrams, story boards (Abernethy and Serfass, 1993), and flow charts (Abernethy and Serfass, 1993; Duden, 1993) contribute to improving school organizations. The PDCA approach and analytical quality tools have improved schools in a variety of areas of instruction, community relations, and school climate.

Over time, educational writers have come to characterize Deming's theories as Total Quality Management (TQM). (See for example, Juran cited in Harris & Harris, 1993; Freeston 1993; Walton 1986). The utility of Deming's work has been expanded by others here and abroad (Hunt, 1993; McClanahan and Wicks, 1993; Scherkenbach, 1992; Akao, 1991, 1990; Marsh, Moran, Nakui, and Hoffherr, 1991; Aguayo, 1990; Gabor, 1990; Brassard, 1989; Eureka and Ryan, 1988; Scholtes, 1988; Ishikawa, 1986; Imai, 1986; Hosotani, 1984). These writers have elaborated and deepened understanding of Deming's Theory of Profound Knowledge and 14 Points, and have expanded the use of analytical tools. Recognizing these contributions to quality improvement theories, educators may effectively adopt the Deming approach to improve schools.

However, the gap in the understanding of quality management between industry and educators raises important questions. Have the educational writers missed key points that would help teachers do their best? Are school administrators focusing on the system, as Deming advocates, in order to improve education?

Or are they, instead, focusing on improving teacher performance without changing the processes, thereby driving fear into the organization (Deming, 1993)? Studies completed by Lilyquist (1995) and Conzemius (1993) explored similar questions.

The educational literature discusses two means of improving schools to meet public expectations. The Effective Schools approach recommends copying good traits and practices. Stampen (1987) suggests Deming's 14 Points are the important traits identified by the Effective Schools research. However, Stampen cites a weakness of that research, namely, not providing a model for implementing improvements. Copying good traits from one setting to another is difficult if conditions vary between the settings (Deming, 1986). According to Deming, improvements come mainly from within the organization: from people who are willing (i.e., intrinsically motivated) and able (i.e., trained in analysis) (Deming, 1993). He argues that only management has the power to change the processes that will allow workers to do their best.

Deriving from the thinking of Deming and the Effective Schools research, Lilyquist's study (1995) found three key factors that affect teachers attitudes toward school improvement. The three factors are educational innovations or changes in organizational structure that:

1. Modify a teacher's rank in the social structure
2. Block teachers from gaining status or place them at risk of losing status
3. Run contrary to what the teacher perceives as his or her vision

These factors agree with Effective Schools research and Deming's theories that *culture* is an important factor in attempting to improve an organization. Both Effective Schools researchers and Deming's theories agree that when organizations change, the whole culture is affected. Effective Schools research argues that creating an effective school becomes a matter of altering the culture (Lezotte, 1987; Purkey and Smith, 1985). Both Deming and Effective Schools researchers hold management responsible for improvement. Purkey and Smith advocate that management mandate key characteristics that will improve the school. But Lezotte (1987) warns that attempting to introduce many characteristics, even of an effective school, may disrupt the culture. Deming (1993, 1986) stresses the need to meet both external and internal customer needs. He recommends helping people in the organization to contribute their best efforts.

Purkey and Smith believe that mandating best practices can be effective if the mandates do not conflict with the factors that affect teachers' attitudes toward school improvement. Lilyquist identified such factors. For example, his research supports the Effective Schools research that a clear mission is important to school improvement. However, methods used in the schools studied to develop a written mission statement fell short of being accepted by all leadership groups. This suggests that the Effective Schools mandate method for improvement may be in conflict with the factors discovered.

Other authors also caution administrators about how to use mandates to improve organizations. The work of Peter Senge (1994, 1990) suggests that managers must adjust the mental models of organizations and individuals, by building a shared vision. Deming (1993), Glasser (1990b, 1984), and Tribus (1990) recommend methods that do not coerce people into change. Deming's Theory of Profound Knowledge and 14 Points of Management use culture to improve an organization. Glasser (1990b) uses his Control Theory to explain why Deming's theory of management has worked in business and industry, and promotes Deming's theories as tools to improve schools. Tribus (1990) offers an example of the successful application of Deming's theories in a school setting. These authors offer managers alternatives to lead change.

There are other variables besides mental models to consider. The diversity of expectations for our schools compounds the problem of adjusting mental models.

The key factors that affect teachers' attitudes toward school improvement support Deming's Theory of Profound Knowledge. These factors add predictive knowledge by suggesting that if management threatens a teacher's vision by violating any single factor, the teacher will react. They enhance the psychological component of Profound Knowledge and provide administrators with key variables to consider when helping teachers do their best.

The strength of Effective Schools research is in suggesting where ineffective schools may look for weakness. However, this approach offers administrators no planning tools, leaving them to guess which characteristic would most improve the school. The strength of Deming's approach to school improvements is its highly developed analytical planning tools. However, Effective Schools researchers criticize Deming's approach for providing few good examples to follow. Deming believed that duplication of best practices from one organization to another was difficult, because each organization is different; however, he supported the effective schools research for the knowledge it provided. Deming claimed that Effective School researchers did not go far enough in the development of improvement methods.

Deming's approach has been criticized because his work was focused on industry and not on educational processes (Bowles, 1993a,b). Lilyquist's study (Chapters 5 and 6) suggested that a political component be added to Deming's Theory of Profound Knowledge, under the categories of "psychology" and "knowledge of systems" for use in education. This book has presented a model (Fig. 4.6) wherein schools must balance both the environment and organizational culture needs (Chapter 3); to accomplish a balance the leadership, strategies, structure, and results dimensions must be aligned (Chapter 4), to help ensure improvements are integrated into the cultures of the school and the community.

THE BALANCE ALIGNMENT MODEL AND THEORY

The Balance Alignment Model (Fig. 4.6) suggests that the perceived results of the results dimension influence the external and internal cultures. When either culture opposes the results, the intensity of the culture's actions is correlated with the influence required to move the school toward the culture's vision. The leadership (leadership dimension) in each culture makes plans (strategic dimension) and acts to change or maintain the organizational structure (structure dimension), to produce the result (results dimension) it desires. The cultures (external and internal environment culture dimension) can change, block, or modify the four process dimensions: leadership, strategy, structure, and/or results (Lilyquist, 1995).

The case studies demonstrate that change may be blocked in any one of the four process dimensions. In Dryden, the restructuring occurred, but informal leadership blocked the administration from carrying out the second stage of restructuring by making leadership powerless. In Elkin, formal leadership developed a strategy for districtwide improvement, but informal leadership blocked the strategy by making it complex, bogging down the system in a complex array of committees. In Skyland, formal leadership developed a strategy and successfully changed the structure, but the conservative group will block the results of the structural change. In all three schools, intended results of the state's third-grade reading test were blocked. Teachers and administration acted to ensure at least a perception of good results. In each example, a leadership's vision was challenged in different ways, suggesting that leadership formal or informal must successfully navigate all four process dimensions to produce a system change. On the other hand, leadership (formal or informal) has an opportunity to block change in each process dimension. The three case studies suggest that nothing really changes, when both cultures perceive that they have protected or made progress toward their visions.

The utility of the Balance Alignment Model is enhanced by knowledge of the effective schools research. Deming's theories, the mental models of Senge and Glasser, and the utilization of political theories and tools applied to education (Bowles, 1993b; Spring, 1993; Mauriel, 1989) are key.

CONCLUDING COMMENTS AND SUGGESTIONS FOR FURTHER RESEARCH

The Balance Alignment Model and theory presented in this book are just that: a model and a theory. They can be further tested, both quantitatively and qualitatively, to determine whether they apply to other elementary schools, institutions of higher learning, businesses, and industries.

A more fully developed theory would include quantitative measures to determine which variables are most likely to help teachers focus on school improvement without having to focus on self-preservation to carry out their visions. This would enable those in leadership roles to work within the cultures of the internal and external environments and monitor progress, keeping a balance between the cultures, avoiding unproductive time spent struggling to return the school to a balanced state. Leaders would be free to help people focus their mental models on a clear vision (Senge, 1994) that met the expectations of both internal and external customers (Deming, 1993; Juran, 1992).

CHAPTER 13

Boundaries

We have discovered a natural sequence of events that people, including teachers, follow to protect their visions of good schools and classrooms. The relationships among these events are illustrated by the Balance Alignment Model, which emphasizes the ways the needs of the organization and the community are balanced. The systemic model aligns leadership, strategy, structure, and results to satisfy and delight both internal and external customers.

As we've seen, communities differ in their tolerance for changes that affect their visions. Dryden's community seemed very tolerant of change, taking action only when major changes occurred. Elkin's community demanded control and resisted all change that might affect the power structure. Skyland's community seemed to have a moderate tolerance for change until one faction viewed the other to be in total control. Teachers, in general, resisted any change that threatened their vision of a good classroom.

TAMPERING

Teachers, administrators, involved parents and community members, state and local officials work hard to improve schools, or at least to protect their visions of good schools and classrooms. Unfortunately, this hard work can be seen as "tampering" with the system when individuals and groups use their "gut feelings" rather than a scientific approach to solve problems. That can unbalance the system. It is this cycle of tampering, using mandate-and-control leadership to create quick-fix solutions to problems, that is placing the "stranglehold" on our schools. As we've seen, people often implement changes without first considering the effects of the change on the total system: External and Internal Environment Cultures, Leadership formal/informal, Strategy, Structure, and Results. Rather than revealing the key patterns that truly threaten their visions, these actions will block change. They make innovations based on "blind faith," using "gut feelings" to "study" the situation and to select a strategy for improvement.

179

They continue to treat special cause problems as common cause problems, and vice versa, and thus view data as a threat rather than an ally. For them, only "gut feelings" serve to gauge an innovation's worth. Thus, people who've made changes never really know by a research study whether their innovations were effective.

If government reports are a valid indication of public satisfaction with school performance, it's clear that our schools are not meeting the needs of their external customers. If the case studies offered by this book are indicative of the general situation for the internal culture, most teachers have good reason to feel threatened by change. "Blind faith" innovation has done little to improve our schools.

As we continue to tamper with the school system, if we make changes that are untested, and if we call for "progress" that cannot be measured, we drive fear into the systemic (known, unknown, and unknowable, visible and invisible) school structure. As fear increases, the culture of the internal environment increases its activities to protect its vision. The more the internal culture protects its vision, the more it widens the gap between its vision and that of the community. A vicious cycle results: Increased mandates drive in increased fear, which forces increased isolation by teachers, which widens the gap between communities and school system. Only we have the power to change the processes that promote tampering and result in widespread dissatisfaction with our schools.

THE CHALLENGES

Theories like the one presented in this book can help people predict the end results of their actions. But theories must be based on information, on results measured before and after action is taken. We all tend to reject information that is contrary to our beliefs, values, norms, and mores. It's a challenge to study a situation and collect information (data) before we make up our minds!

It's even more difficult to slow down and work within the boundaries of a problem. Boundaries can seem restrictive, when they run counter to our beliefs. Yet if we do not respect known boundaries, we are not likely to be able to fully implement innovations, or to improve a situation. In this book, we've considered three case studies of barriers to school improvement: political structures, culture and individual beliefs, actions of formal and informal leadership, strategies, common patterns of action that occur externally and internally, and effects of results on cultures. Each of these cases contradicts the belief that administrators can mandate change and receive an obedient response. But whether or not we accept this, we can see that operating via mandates is not improving our schools. The challenge is to use knowledge like this, which suggests that something we hold "sacred" is in error.

First, we must open our minds so that the pictures in our albums, our mental models, our visions, have an opportunity to change. Unless we change how we view the local school and the world, our actions will continue to produce the same results. Even though the solution is difficult, we must choke down personal anger, accept reality, and working toward meaningful school improvement.

References

P. E. Abernethy and R. W. Serfass, "One District's Quality Improvement Story," *Educational Leadership* 50(3)(1993):14–17.

R. Aguayo, *Dr. Deming: The American Who Taught the Japanese about Quality* (New York: Fireside, 1990).

Y. Akao, *Quality Function Deployment: Integrating Customer Requirements into Product Design* (Cambridge: Productivity Press, 1990).

Y. Akao, *Hoshin Kanri: Policy Deployment for Successful TQM* (Cambridge: Productivity Press, 1991).

J. Andrade & H. Ryley, "A Quality Approach to Writing Assessment," *Educational Leadership* 50(3)(1993):22–23.

B. Audette and B. Algozzine, "Free and Appropriate Education for All Students: Total Quality and the Transformation of American Public Education," *Remedial and Special Education* 13(6)(1992):8–18.

J. Barker, *Future Edge: Discovering the New Paradigms of Success* (New York: Morrow, 1992).

J. Bellanca, "Can Quality Circles Work in Classrooms of the Gifted?," *Roper Review* 6(4)(1984):199–200.

A. Blankstein, "Applying the Deming Corporate Philosophy to Restructuring," *The Educational Digest* 58(6)(1993):28–32.

J. Bonstingl, "The Quality Revolution in Education," *Educational Leadership* 50(3)(1993):4–9.

B. D. Bowles "Field Research Design and Methodologies in Educational Administration: Lecture Notes," Department of Educational Administration, University of Wisconsin-Madison (1993a).

B. D. Bowles, "The Politics of Education: Lecture Notes," Department of Educational Administration, University of Wisconsin-Madison (1993b).

R. Brandt, "On Deming and School Quality: A Conversation with Enid Brown," *Educational Leadership* 50(3)(1993a):28–31.

R. Brandt, "On Restructuring Roles and Relationships: A Conversation with Phil Schlechty," *Educational Leadership* 51(2)(1993b):8–11.

M. Brassard, *The Memory Jogger Plus+* (Methuen: GOAL/QPC, 1989).

M. Cohn & R. A. Rossmiller, "Research on Effective Schools: Implications for Less Developed Countries," *Comparative Education Review* 31(3)(1987):377–399.

W. Conzemius, "An Exploratory Study of the Principles of Deming's Theory of Management in Public Schools Involved in Reform," Unpublished doctoral dissertation, University of Wisconsin-Madison (1993).

W. E. Deming, *Out of the Crisis* (Cambridge: Massachusetts Institute of Technology, 1986).

W. E. Deming, *The New Economics: For Industry, Government, Education* (Cambridge: Massachusetts Institute of Technology, 1993).

L. Dobyns and C. Crawford-Mason, *Thinking about Quality: Progress, Wisdom, and the Deming Philosophy* (New York: Time Books, 1994).

N. Duden, "A Movement from Effective to Quality," *The School Administrator* 50(5)(1993):18–31.

W. Eureka and N. Ryan, *The Customer-Driven Company: Managerial Perspectives on QFD* (Dearborn: American Supplier Institute,, 1988).

K. Freeston, "Getting Started with TQM," *Educational Leadership* 50(3)(1993):10–11.

A. Gabor, *The Man Who Discovered Quality* (New York: Penguin Group, 1990).

B. G. Glaser and A. L. Strauss, *The Discovery of Grounded Theory: Strategies for Qualitative Research* (Hawthorne, NY: Aldine de Gruyter, 1967).

W. Glasser, *Control Theory: A New Explanation of How We Control Our Lives* (New York: Harper & Row, 1984).

W. Glasser, "The Quality School," *Phi Delta Kappan* 71(6)(1990a):425–435.

W. Glasser, *The Quality School: Managing Students without Coercion* (New York: Harper & Row, 1990b)

H. Goldhamer and E. Shils, "Types of Power and Status," *The American Journal of Sociology* 45(9) (1939):171–182.

M. F. Harris and R. C. Harris, "Glasser Comes to a Rural School," *Educational Leadership* 50(3) (1993):18–21.

M. M. Hmaidan, "The Characteristics of Effective Secondary Schools in Jordan," unpublished doctoral dissertation, University of Wisconsin-Madison (1991).

M. Holt, "The Educational Consequences of W. Edwards Deming," *Phi Delta Kappan* 74(5)(1993): 382–388.

K. Hosotani, *Japanese Quality Concepts; An Overview* (White Plains: Quality Resources, 1984).

V. Hunt, *Managing for Quality: Integrating Quality and Business Strategy* (Homewood, IL: Business One Irwin, 1993).

M. Imai, *Kaizen* (New York: McGraw-Hill, 1986).

K. Ishikawa, *Guide to Quality Control* (Minato-ku, Tokyo: Asian Productivity Organization, 1986).

B. Joiner, *Fourth Generation Management: The New Business Consciousness* (New York: McGraw–Hill, 1994).

J. Juran, *Juran on Quality By Design: The New Steps for Planning Quality into Goods and Services* (New York: The Free Press, 1992).

R. Kaufman and A. Hirumi, "Ten Steps to 'TQM Plus,'" *Educational Leadership* 50(3)(1993):33–34.

L. W. Lezotte (producer), *Effective School: Premises, Concepts and Characteristics* (videotape) (Okemos, MI: Effective School Products, 1987).

L. W. Lezotte (producer), *Questions Teachers Have about Implementing Effective Schools at the Elementary Level* (videotape). (Okemos, MI: Effective School Products, (1990a).

L. W. Lezotte (producer), *Implementing Effective Schools at the Elementary Level* (videotape) (Okemos, MI: Effective School Products, (1990b).

L. W. Lezotte, *Creating the Total Quality Effective School* (Okemos, MI: Effective School Products, (1992a).

L. W. Lezotte (speaker), *Larry Lezotte on the Total Quality Effective School* (cassette recording) (Oxford: National Staff Development Council, 1992b).

J. Lilyquist, "Factors Affecting Teacher Attitudes toward School Improvement," Unpublished doctoral dissertation, University of Wisconsin-Madison (1995).

P. Macchia, "Assessing Educational Processes Using Total-Quality-Management Measurement Tools," *Educational Technology* 33(3)(1993):48–54.

T. Mackey and K. Mackey, "Think Quality! The Deming Approach Does Work in Libraries," *Library Journal* 117(9)(1992):57–61.

S. Marsh, J. Moran, S. Nakui, and G. Hoffherr, *Facilitating and Training in Quality Function Deployment* (Methuen: GOAL/QPC, 1991).

J. J. Mauriel, *Strategic Leadership: Creating and Sustaining Change* (San Francisco: Jossey–Bass, 1989).

D. McCarty and C. Ramsey, "Community Power, School Board Structure, and the Role of the Chief School Administrator," *Educational Administration Quarterly* 4(2)(1968):19–33.

E. McClanahan and C. Wicks, *Future Force: Kids That Want to Can and Do!: A Teachers Handbook* (Redlands: PACT Publishing, 1993).

A. K. B. Mohd Nor, "Characteristics of Effective Rural Secondary Schools in Malaysia," Unpublished doctoral dissertation, University of Wisconsin-Madison (1989).

S. C. Purkey and M. S. Smith, "Effective Schools: A Review," *The Elementary School Journal* 85(3)(1983):427–452.

S. C. Purkey and M. S. Smith, "School Reform: The District Policy Implications of Effective School Literature," *The Elementary School Journal* 85(3)(1985):353–387.

S. Rankin, "Total Quality Management: Implications for Educational Assessment," *NASSP Bulletin* 76(545)(1992):66–76.

L. Rhodes, "On the Road to Quality," *Educational Leadership* 49(6)(1992):76–80.

W. W. Scherkenbach, *The Deming Route to Quality and Productivity* (Washington, DC: CEEPress Books, 1992).

M. Schmoker and R. B. Wilson, "Transforming Schools through Total Quality Education," *Phi Delta Kappan* 74(5)(1993):389–395.

P. Scholtes, *The Team Handbook* (Madison: Joiner Associates, 1988).

P. M. Senge, *The Fifth Discipline* (New York: Doubleday, 1990).

P. M. Senge, *The Fifth Discipline Fieldbook: Strategies and Tools for Building a Learning Organization* (New York: Doubleday, 1994).

R. C. Shirley. and J. K. Caruters, *Strategic Planning for Higher Education*, Presented at the annual meeting of the American Association of State Colleges and Universities, San Antonio (1979).

J. Spring, *Conflict of Interest*, 2nd ed. (White Plains: Longman Publishing Group, 1993).

J. O. Stampen, "Improving the Quality of Education: W. Edwards Deming and Effective Schools," *Contemporary Education Review* 3(3)(1987):423–433.

J. O. Stampen, "The Theory and Practice of Educational Planning: Lecture Notes," Department of Educational Administration, University of Wisconsin-Madison (1992).

J. O. Stampen (ed.), Draft untitled article, Department of Educational Administration, University of Wisconsin-Madison (1994, January).

M. Tribus, "The Application of Quality Management Principles in Education, at Mt. Edgecumbe High School, Sitka, Alaska," Unpublished manuscript (1990).

United States, *National Commission on Excellence in Education: A Nation at Risk: the Imperative for Educational Reform: A Report to the Nation and Secretary of Education, United States, Department of Education* (Washington, DC: Superintendent of Documents, GPO, 1983).

United States Congress, House. *Congressional Record*, 103rd Cong., 2nd sess., March 21,1994, H.R. 1804 (Goals 2000) (1994).

V. Vertiz, "A Look at the Curriculum Management Audit Applying Dr. Deming's Principles for System Transformation," *Education* 113(2)(1992):210–214.

M. Walton, *The Deming Management Method* (New York: Putnam Publishing Group, 1986).

Index